STREAM Publishing,
Unit 40,
The Enterprise Centre,
Treorchy,
Wales,
CF42 6EJ

Scripture quotations are from the Mew International Version of
the Bible. Copyright C 1973, 1978, International Bible Society.
Published by Hodder & Stoughton.

ISBN No. 0-9545011-0-1

Printed in Wales by Allprint Limited

PREFACE

"If you really keep the royal law found in Scripture, 'Love your neighbour as yourself', you are doing right".

James 2:8

INDEX

Chapter 1

AND SO IT BEGAN

Everyone knows that Television blurs the senses but this was TV unlike anything I'd ever watched before. I was not unused to examining my heart but never before had I looked at it from the inside. I was on the operating table in Withenshaw hospital in Manchester undergoing a procedure called Cardio ablation. Level with my chest was a screen to stop me from seeing the lower half of my body and to my left were TV monitors. I was wide awake and could see and feel the instruments that were inside my heart to isolate the weakness so that the weakness could be ablated. Never had I been through anything like this. In a sense the operation, as I see it now, had begun a few months earlier perhaps several years earlier but we can start in North Wales.

We were in Prestatyn in North Wales and were making our first trip home from Africa in two years. Even after just two years, it was quite an adjustment to get used to the pace and way of life in the UK. We were attending the annual UK conference of the Elim Pentecostal Church and it was a time of high excitement for us, particularly seeing many old friends and colleagues. We had with us at the conference Ayhubu Mgweno from Tanzania and Simon Githigi from Kenya two men who had become very dear to us.

Ayhubu was the chairman of the Elim works in Tanzania and Simon his counterpart in Kenya. I was just enjoying the sense of God and worshipping amongst the wider Elim church. During the afternoons I was attending what is referred to as 'The Business Sessions' where the ministers and lay leaders meet to discuss business and the way forward for the movement. On the Wednesday afternoon we were discussing finances with regard to evangelism and missions in general. I felt troubled in my spirit. I had recently been with the two men from East Africa in Rwanda amongst the aftermath of genocide and my overall perspective had been heightened by what I had experienced in East Africa. I felt that I needed to bring a point of view into the meeting of some 450 leaders but having never spoken out at a business session at the conference before, I decided to wait, ponder over my thoughts and pray.

The next day we were discussing pensions and I knew in

my spirit that God wanted me to speak. I handed in my slip *(the normal procedure)* and sat back down feeling unusually nervous. I waited patiently but wasn't called by Wynne Lewis who was chairing the session. I interpreted it to mean that God didn't want me to speak and went back to my seat somewhat embarrassed. However, a little later I was called and given a warm welcome as this was my first leave from the mission field.

As I began to address this large gathering of leaders I fumbled at first, I went on to genuinely thank those who worked behind the scenes with pensions and such but I wanted to draw attention to a man who had served the movement for 41 years in Tanzania - often without any money at all. Ayhubu Mgweno owned nothing that we would consider valuable. He didn't own his own home had no car, no computer and nothing that we would consider a pension. Even though he was nearing retirement he still travelled around East Africa by bus visiting different parts of the work. 'He has nothing of real value in this world materially as I have but I 'm in awe of him' I remarked, my voice rising and full of emotion. I drew more attention to him and asked that we might gain some perspective.

After about ten minutes I finished and sat down - the place was hushed and the presence of God tangible. I can only describe what happened next as remarkable. Many commented afterwards that God's presence was awesome and that it was a defining moment for the movement.

Ayhubu was called to address the gathering. Into the dramatic hush, he merely whispered, 'I think everything has already been said.' With this I was as surprised as anyone to find myself prostrate on the floor - I was weeping aloud and uncontrollably. Then our incoming General Superintendent John Glass asked if he could clean Ayhubu's shoes with his handkerchief. Many people began to weep and prostrate themselves.

One man came from the back of the auditorium and took off his shoes and wrist-watch and placed it on the platform at the front. He was followed by a gentle stream of people laying down money and private possessions. Business was now postponed as Simon Githigi addressed the crowd. God's presence filled the building. In that short period of time Ayhubu was honoured by God with several thousand pounds that would buy him land, build him a house and provide a pension. In addition the plight of our overseas workers would be reviewed. He had made no appeal and sold no merchandise but God knew his plight. I had had no idea that God was going to do such a thing. I was merely hurting in my heart with regard to what I knew to be the reality of service for our third world colleagues. When you consider the average wage in Tanzania is around $130 per annum you will get some idea of what I had experienced.

What happened that day to bring the manifest presence of God into that meeting? I cannot say for sure but obviously I have analysed it over and over in my mind and feel that

I have some answers.

This book is the result of a long and painful journey but will shed some light on what God has shown me. Even though I was indirectly involved that day I have to honestly say that in all my time in the church and ministry I have never experienced anything like the presence of God that filled that building. I had experienced God moving powerfully before but this was different – it was tangible and an obvious lasting work was in motion. Certainly in my own life this has proven to be so.

Meanwhile, I could have no idea then of what was to follow in the next few months. The following few pages are a brutal account of what went on and the lessons learned.

Chapter 2

AN ACHING HEART

After a great summer ministering around the Elim churches in the UK and spending as much time as possible with family and friends we returned to Africa on the 2nd of August. As we landed in Nairobi it was a good feeling to see the sights and smell the scent that is peculiar to East Africa. It had been wonderful to be home in the UK but we agreed that Africa felt like home now.

We had so much to catch up on with colleagues and friends in the ex-pat community, so much work to do into the future. Our role was to oversee the Elim work throughout East Africa which consisted of Tanzania, Rwanda, Uganda, Kenya, East Congo and Burundi. Our area was many times bigger than Britain and this in itself made the work seem impossible. It was an endless stream of dire human need - at times incomprehensible to our western values and lifestyles. The security issues make it almost impossible to live out some romantic dream that we should live as the Africans do in the Bush. We were working amongst the poorest of the poor but living in a nice home, even by western standards.

There are many paradoxes in Africa; it was once described as a lot of lovely people doing unspeakable things to one another. Many times I had lost myself walking and praying around our home town of Arusha, contemplating the enigma that is Africa. It can lift you up and it can bring you down swiftly, suddenly and destructively.

Because we had relative wealth we had learned to live with 24 hours haskari *(guards)* on our fortress like property – we also had guard dogs roaming, all this to protect us from those we had come to serve and to reach – hmmm... It was something that one got used to eventually. The truth was that without these measures you **would be** violently robbed. It was not merely a possibility it was a certainty! As a family man – my children Chris and Beth were at that time, 8 and 6 respectively - one could not take such risks. Desperation and the ease in which a person can get hold of guns is quite a potent recipe. Many of our friends had suffered armed robbery.

There were so many desperate needs surrounding us that we were often completely overwhelmed. The queue of needy folk was like an endless stream - exasperating. It seemed like we had to put a guard around our hearts so that we could maintain some normality as a young family.

Often I would be away for weeks at a time driving endless miles to reach various parts of our work. What a variety: I could find myself in a refugee camp one week, an executive meeting the next and famine relief soon after. Through it all I was never quite sure that this was God's *bull's eye* for my life. Overwhelming is not an adjective that is too emphatic for what we faced. Despite all this misery, it is true to say that Africa does get in your blood; she is like a lover who lifts you up with delightful promises only to dump you suddenly. The missionary feels much undervalued in East Africa in the sense that whatever endeavours he undertakes on behalf of the indigenous population it is only what is expected and this is usually swiftly followed by a request for more – the begging bowl is swiftly emptied. It often seemed to me that I was not simply trying to meet the needs of a village but rather that of several nations.

The following are two accounts from my diary that show the ecstasy, the elation and the frustrations of working in Africa.

11th March 2000, Ngara refugee camp, Western Tanzania

> *'This was one of the most amazing days of my life. We visited the refugee camp at Ngara. Both the trip and the time spent there was fantastic and memorable! The crossing of the bridge over the Kagere River where so many genocide victims were disposed of was a stark reminder of what went on here. The tremendous welcome of the Burundian pastors and people in the camp (they had been waiting five days for us) was*

remarkable, the great anointing of God breaking out
spontaneously on the people. The sights we saw. The
miracle of getting back across a closed border and the
singing and fellowship in the packed vehicle on the
way back – what a day! A million thanks Lord for the
way this day has affected my heart.'

10th January 2000, Soroti, Uganda

'The demands of this job are far too great. The Africans
are looking for an administrator to sponsor them and
their expectations far exceed mine or Elim's ability to
meet them. How can one person even begin to
administer this major operation?

Many times when I try to make clear how I feel to the
Africans their response is non-plussed. I don't think
that they can begin to understand how we Wazungu
(white men) feel. I am not even sure that culturally
(with all that has gone on historically in Colonial
days) that they want to love us. We can be used by
them. The problem is we do not have anything like the
money they think we have. Even if we did it would be
morally wrong to dish it out like candy. Our only hope
is to build strong churches in the cities and give some
indigenous example to the rest of the work. Another
problem is that we are not in a place long enough to
have any kind of relationship with our people. We flit
in and flit out – doling the shillings as we go. The

shillings are never enough thus, greatly undervaluing all that we are seeking to do. The mission field of East Africa has become a pariah even to the degree that the pioneer missionaries, who gave so much, are almost blamed for the attitudes of the present day Christians. 'They gave us something material in order to preach the gospel to us', some Africans reason. Nowadays, that mindset is so engrained as to be a very big 'stronghold'.

What can be done when the African church (in some instances) will sell out to the highest bidder among the organisations from the West? The truth is there are some naïve and, may I say, unscrupulous ministries that will offer 'the candy' in order to add to the books.

There can be no doubt that we in Elim East Africa are facing a formidable stronghold. At present I do not think that we have either the resources or the personnel to bring this thing down. Accordingly, the frustrations are enormous. We certainly need more resources but surely they must be provided indigenously? I must have an understanding of what can be expected with regard to tithes and offerings into the head offices of each country. I may not fully understand the ins and outs of all that this entails but the principle remains: Elim in East Africa must be built on Scriptural principles and not be swayed by preserving circumstances.

We must also develop communications (at this time we do not have even one computer amongst all our workers in all of Elim East Africa). There should at least be a network uniting all of the head offices. We should also consider putting short-term workers into each head office to observe and to minister under the supervision of Elim UK. Two week visits can be very productive but may also leave people with a false impression and therefore be counter-productive.

As it stands we simply do not have either the practical or human resources to advance. It is a full-time job simply to maintain. We cannot and should not underestimate the spiritual resistance and subsequent pressure that this places on one person. We should project by faith but can only manage to work within the set parameters that present circumstances allow. Advancement that does not have its origins in God is no real advancement at all and will at some stage, be paid for by someone. God is only interested in reality and not how something may look from external observations. The fact remains Elim in East Africa has expectations that far exceeds the ability of Elim in the UK to meet them. Each country is constantly presenting needs that far outweigh the entire budget for the whole region. To compound this, most of these needs are genuine and, in some cases, desperate. We could spend our entire budget, our entire salary and still not scratch the surface in meeting one need in one country. Such is the frustration!

We cannot single-handedly solve the problems of what is, after all, a region of third world countries. Of course we do not act alone but I think it behoves us to ask serious questions of what does God expect from Elim within the complexities of all that is East Africa. The shear geographical size of the region (many times bigger than Britain); the poor, at best, non existent at worst, communications and the extreme poverty ought to cause us to face a re-think. The 'shaking of the tree' mentality is coped by most only at a village level (literally). We have to cope with it at a multi-national level. Only one who has faced the African way of shaking the tree can begin to understand the pressure that this brings to bare. Overwhelming is definitely the right word!' Help!

Like I have just said, my life moved from feelings of elation to feelings of great frustration. This is normal for missionary work and is one of the things that can make it different from ministry in the West. This was certainly the case for me with the role that I had.

As we progressed through the month of August, I was feeling fresh and encouraged and made the long journey down to Dar es Salaam in Tanzania. I went to meet my friend and supervisor from Wales, Denis Phillips. We had a few meetings in Dar before passing through Tanga and setting off on our long drive to Arusha, to prepare for our first East African Leaders conference. We had a great sense that we were breaking new ground and God was moving on our hearts through the deep conversations we were having.

On the 21st of August our Elim leaders arrived from Uganda, Kenya, Rwanda and one from the refugee camp, that I had visited in Ngara in Western Tanzania. Back in Arusha it was with excitement and enthusiasm that Denis and I ministered to the 20 or so key leaders that had gathered together. The main theme of my teaching was taken from Ephesians 3:14-21, while Denis brought revelation about the gifts of the Spirit. Not for the first time, Denis and I were in tandem and tremendous things were happening. We finished on the Saturday and after loving farewells almost collapsed with exhaustion! On Sunday afternoon we met with our so called, "afternoon group" who were, in the main, a gathering of fellow missionaries. As Denis ministered effectively into this close group of friends - little did I know that a few hours later I would be unconscious!

The palpitations that I had been suffering kept me awake that night and I went to the toilet at about 1:30am feeling weak and faint. As I was leaving the bathroom I collapsed and lay in an unconscious state for sometime. I came round with a bloodied head and awoke my wife Debbie - she phoned a missionary doctor who was a good friend and speedily drove me to a clinic in town where I spent the night. I was assured that I hadn't had a heart attack but that I had a severe irregular heartbeat. This was confirmed a couple of days later as I underwent extensive tests in Nairobi.

Dr Patel the consultant informed me that as I had both a fast and a slow heartbeat it was fairly complicated and the treatment would require both medication and a pacemaker - the medication to slow the heart down and the pacemaker to make sure it wouldn't slow down too much. The decision was made to come back to the UK. A few days later we were back in Blackpool with Deb's parents and soon after I was taken in to Blackpool's Victoria Hospital where my condition stabilized. After a few days I was released and for several weeks I went back and forth to the hospital and eventually I was advised to have the afore mentioned operation called Cardioablation. As I was feeling fairly good at this stage it was decided that we would return to Africa and later on, I would come back to the UK to have my operation. Thus, we met with our Regional Superintendent Denis Phillips and our Missions Director Brian Edwards. The meeting went well and it was decided that we would indeed return to Africa and it was with some excitement and not a little relief that we drove back to Blackpool.

That evening I went to see my GP and he told me that my consultant had communicated that he wanted to change my medication from Sotolol to Flacanide. He issued me with a prescription and dutifully I began to take the new medication - little did I know that a near fatal mistake had been made.

The following night I felt my heart beat slowing to a point that I knew my life was in danger. The next morning I called my GP who said that I had to persevere on the new medication. By Friday I was in a terrible state and was amazed to find out from my Consultant that I should have come off the Sotolol two days before I started the Flacanide and that in Blackpool the procedure was to go in as a day patient to be monitored on the Flacanide.

By Sunday I was back in Victoria Hospital as an emergency case - my heartbeat was between 180-200 beats per minute in the resting position. Later in the week it slowed to a dangerous 22 beats per minute, yet through it all I felt I was in God's hands and at peace. After nine days I was transferred to Withenshaw hospital in Manchester where I underwent the Cardio Ablation procedure. It was one of the strangest experiences of my life.

The procedure involves passing five tubes into veins in the groin - one being in the main artery. Through these tubes instruments are passed into the heart in an attempt to locate the weakness. Once the weakness or extra passage is found it is then burnt out or cauterised. All of this takes place while the patient is wide awake. It is possible to watch this entire procedure on screens at the side of one's head. Not nice! It was however, effective, but what happened in the following months became a nightmare as my whole system seemed to dysfunction.

To begin with I began to suffer chronic insomnia to the

point that I could no longer sleep naturally. I could not even cat-nap or fall asleep even for five minutes. I quickly became exhausted and was sure that I was dying. In addition I would sweat profusely for no apparent reason; even taking a warm drink would cause me to be drenched through perspiration. Later my digestive system could not handle food and I began to pass meals undigested. During this period I suffered different pains all around my body including migraine and I was rapidly losing weight. The period over Christmas was a sad and desperate time. In the early hours of Christmas Day I penned the following words in my journal.

> *My beloved family how I love you all, and need you, I can't begin to tell you the torture and torment that is going on inside me at the moment. I have taken so much for granted and now it seems that I have lost it. How I plead with God to give me another chance to get back to normal living. My mind is in such turmoil. My need of sleep and rest is obvious. Deb you have been my dream girl from when we first met - how sorry I am that it has come to this! What a partner you have proven to be, God knows I never deserved somebody like you. Thank you for standing by me through these troubled days. How fortunate I am - I ask you to remember the real me and pray that we will have a miracle of restoration. How I wish I could be me and join in the Christmas festivities wholeheartedly - my lack of sleep is dampening my enthusiasm because of the prospects of tomorrow.*

Only God knows if there is a way forward out of this mess? I need help and am so grateful to have a loving family around me. You have all been better than words could describe. The fruit shown by your mum and dad have proven them to be giants in my sight. Thank you Chris and Beth I plead with God that he will allow me to share in your tomorrows - you are fantastic my angels. Words cannot describe how I feel about you all. I have been very fortunate as I look back and think about the amazing times that God has given us. Oh that he will give us more in the future. In the service on Christmas Day as I sat at the back of the church I was so proud to see your ministry Deb - you really have something special in God and you looked so radiant. The hat makes you look very beautiful indeed (you have just told me to write good things - I was as you can see) it is a privilege to be your husband. You know that I have always felt that but certainly during these days of my illness I have so appreciated every touch - every chance to hold hands - every cuddle.

Remember when we first met and went out, how precious every touch was, every look, every letter (where are they?). We can safely say that we have never lost our romance, have we? It has always given me a tingle to be in your arms - even the slightest touch has been precious to me always. And the joy of producing two fantastic children together - surely they are amazing? (Wouldn't any proud father say that?). Chris and Beth I just want to write the words, I LOVE

*YOU. Deb, I want to write these words, I LOVE
YOU. I have to nip myself when I consider that I am
married to you. I mean it from the bottom of my heart
when I say that you are, to me, the greatest, most ideal
woman in the world. That is how I have always seen it.
Every parting has been a desperate time until we were
back together again. God grant us tomorrow and may
our tomorrows be even greater than our yesterdays!*

I was writing as a man who had lost all hope *(I have since
learned that a Christian is never truly in that position)* and
really felt that each day would be my last. I can happily
testify that God answered that prayer from a desperate
child. It is hard now to read that entry into my journal
without tears welling up.

One thing I have realised since my illness is that I thought,
during it, that I was thinking normally and using my
usual analytical thought processes. I now know that I was
not. The worst thought was that God was punishing me.
My mind was in turmoil and I was under enormous stress.
Consider that our home and possessions were still 5,000
miles away in Tanzania. We simply had no security and no
direction for the future. The stress became visibly obvious
on Debbie and from time to time the children would
tearfully ask, 'Daddy when are we going back to Africa?' I
simply felt that death was imminent and worse that I
would end up in hell! My mind was so stressed. We were
in turmoil and I felt like I was under pressure, literally, 24
hours a day. I didn't want to die but I seriously thought

that my family would be better off without me.

On December 28th Debbie – in quiet desperation phoned Denis Phillips to ask if he could help me. That day I travelled down to Swansea to be the guest and patient of Denis and his wife Ronaldine. Once again, I was about to be overwhelmed by love and kindness. They gave their time, energy and decision making over to me – this included setting the daily agenda and even choosing the menu. I was experiencing God's unconditional love through people at precisely the time when I thought I didn't deserve it. Daily, Denis took me to spots around South Wales that had become familiar to Deb and me over the years. One day we went down to the seafront at Mumbles and the next to the lovely resort of Tenby.

Another of the days that will stick in my memory forever was a day when I noticed that the Chinese meal I had eaten the evening before had been passed through my system undigested – this fact served to compound my fears. As Denis and I walked on the beach at Oxwich Bay on the Gower I reminisced of the times that Deb, the children and I had enjoyed there during better times. I felt just like I imagined the condemned man must feel on death row. I felt that my life was over and I could only plead inwardly that God would restore me and give me another chance (*my frame of mind at the time didn't really allow for this possibility but I have now been back to Oxwich Bay on several occasions with my family*) I was a desperate man!

On New Years Eve in 2001, I sat in Denis's home like a zombie. Denis continued to fill my mind with positive thoughts but it was hard to take them onboard. After about a week Deb and the children arrived. I went to see them wearing a new haircut and dressed in a new suit that Denis had bought me. I took Deb for a romantic meal at the Watermill restaurant – she was looking particularly lovely and that night was one of the most amazing of my life. It was like our first date. In the midst of our prevailing circumstances we could only trust God for the future – on this occasion my trust had to go way beyond my human hope.

We spent the next few days at the Phillips' home counting every moment as precious. During those days I was shocked when Denis asked me if I would like to preach at the church we had pastored in Porth on the coming Sunday. I had not preached for months and initially I thought it impossible. Nevertheless, Denis convinced me that Porth had asked me to go and I eventually agreed.

As Sunday morning arrived *(after a sleepless night)* I wondered what on earth had inspired me to agree to go and preach! I felt awful on the journey and as we entered the Rhondda Valley via Trebanog memories of the nine happy years we had spent there came flooding back. Tears welled up in my eyes as we arrived in Porth and we were given a tremendous reception from the folk in the church. When the time came to preach I spoke from the heart on the subject of 'suffering' and at the end of the sermon many people came forward to pray and lay hands on me for healing. Although I didn't realise it at that time, we had just experienced our "beginning point."

After the meeting we went for lunch to the home of John and Jill Price who had been like surrogate parents to us over the years. John had been an Elder for many years in the church in Porth and, along with Jill, epitomises the outliving of the Christian message – they are truly dependable people with massive integrity. As a family we had grown to love them dearly, they were like rocks to us. After the usual scrumptious lunch at the Price household I asked John if we could speak in private. He became one of the three people that I opened up my heart to and confessed my known sins. I was convinced that I needed to carry out the injunction in the book of James 5:16,

"confess your sins to one another and you will be healed."

I thought that maybe this was the obstacle to me being restored *(as previously stated I was so desperate and feeling that I had even been abandoned by God)* so if it was the obstacle I was going to do all that was in my power to remove it. That afternoon I went through sins some of which had been committed up to fifteen years previously and confessed years before but I wanted to make sure that I was forgiven. Poor John sat and listened and tried to bring comfort to me. I was a haunted person and felt prepared to go through any humbling just to recover from my *(imagined)* fallen position in Christ.

I didn't know then, as I do now, that sin and law come at the believer hand-in-hand. The effect of the law on those who have little conscience has only a silent, unknown yet devastating affect, whereas, it serves to bring immediate condemnation into the believers life - one who is in reality no longer under law. The guilt, turmoil and torment of the Christian often has no substance outside of a believers thoughts but the thoughts can be so powerful that they take life upon themselves – I have learnt that this is true in a positive sense as well as a negative one. The law has its most devastating effect in the thought lives of those who are striving to be, "Pure in heart." We left the Rhondda that day oblivious that God was about to perform an amazing twist in this ongoing tale.

Later in January Debbie and I went to meet with our superiors again. This time we were told that we would not be going back to Tanzania (*I was already reconciled to this*). The news was devastating for Debbie - I think she had not come to terms with what was, at the time, a foregone conclusion. It was a dreadful meeting at which I remained speechless while my darling wife broke her heart. As far as I was concerned she was suffering because of God's displeasure with me.

I felt like I was an impostor, how much I needed to learn some basic foundational truths about the nature of God, even though I had been in the ministry for many years! In short my soul had not been restored!

As the meeting concluded we made a swift decision to travel back to Wales to stay with our friends, Andrew and Cath Smith. In later days we would recount how I sat in their lounge once again resembling a zombie. After another sleepless night I paced about the room trying to concentrate in prayer. Eventually, I felt that God was speaking to me in my thoughts *(the manner in which I had been accustomed to over the years)* saying that we should move back to the Rhondda Valley. The second thing I heard was that we would have to climb a mountain but when we arrived at the summit we would be at a place that few people arrive at.

Debbie and I chatted over this latest revelation and somehow it took root within us. At the very least we could settle back into a familiar area where many of our friends lived and where our children had spent their earliest years. Later that day I spoke to Denis Phillips and he said he would support our decision. It was the first day of a remarkable chain of events - we had definitely boarded the vehicle of recovery.

In early February we moved back to South Wales and stayed with our friends Howard and Teg Evans at their spacious home in Pontypridd. Howard and Teg offered us wonderful hospitality and kindness. We quickly settled Chris and Beth in new schools and I began some voluntary work with my friend Phil Davies who is the Communications Director of Newport Rugby Club. Phil, along with Carl Brettle, had formed a Christian company to facilitate the growing opportunities afforded by the Internet.

It was an exciting time and by now I was getting at least some sleep due to the effects of a previously untried sleeping tablet called Zopliclone. We began to settle back into the valleys. I was still living one day at a time but seeds of faith had sprung in my heart. I began to receive hope through the means of faith. As the days went by I began to deal with things completely by faith. In other words I disregarded my feelings, learning that though my situation was the reality that I could, through faith, attack it with a higher reality.

A few months earlier on 29th November 2000, I had written these words in my diary:

> *Trying circumstances sometimes look as if they combine for a person's destruction - they do not, they only combine for the destruction of the self-life and then the working out of the Christ-life from within him.*

Later I would learn that, if we believe the truth, obey the commands and claim the promises then eventually our **position** in Christ will overcome our **condition** in the world!

Gradually *(though not without setbacks)* this began to happen. What a lesson: unless you are certain of your position in Christ it is highly likely that you will give in to your condition. I needed to understand that 'amazing grace' as opposed to just grace as I had understood it would radically change my outlook and, as a result, my life and the lives of multitudes of people. I learned that the important thing was to make contact with God until you can find what I describe as a **beginning point** and then to walk hand in hand with the Lord until the victory is manifest. What hope is born in understanding that simple procedure?

So here we were settling back into the Rhondda Valley but still our home and possessions were in Tanzania. One Saturday I was invited to share a little bit at a Prayer School led by Jenny Grant who had worked with us in Porth for a number of years. It was there that one of several domestic miracles took place. I was approached by a man called Allan Jones who was one of the leaders at Providence Church further up the valley. He told me that the church had a house that was empty and that we could move in straight away if we wanted to. I told him we were interested and after viewing the property we moved in. As I write this we have lived rent free in the house for two years. About this time we were also supplied with a car *(free of charge)* from Phil Davies - things were indeed looking up or at least some one was *looking down.*

As my health improved we began to feel confident to go back to Tanzania and settle our affairs there. By faith we decided to plan to go in June. However, before this happened something amazing was about to happen. The church we had formerly pastored in Porth was experiencing some difficulties with division in thinking amongst the leadership *(I mention this in relation to what will follow)*. We had previously known little about this but could see that the situation was grave. Many of the people who were involved had been with us during our time at Porth and the whole situation between the present pastor and some of the leaders was in danger of splitting the church. It was difficult to sit back and watch this happen but we no longer had a say in matters and I had been too ill to even think about it. As a few weeks passed by the situation worsened when out of the blue Paul Edwards the minister announced that he was leaving to take up a new position in Sheffield. No-one had had any idea that this was about to happen. Immediately, I was asked to return as pastor.

It would be possible to read all kinds of things into these happenings but God knows that no one in the church, least of all Debbie and I, had any foreknowledge of these events. In May 2001 I was inaugurated back into the pastorate. As Deb and I had never lost our love for the Welsh Valleys doubled with the fact that I am a Welsh speaker - we can only look back and ascertain that God took hold of our lives and worked through the events that you have just read about.

On 17th June we went back to Arusha and had a memorable time seeing our friends and tidying up our affairs after our emergency departure some nine months before. I felt well and was greatly looking forward to our new challenge in Porth.

I have a good imagination but I could never have written the script for what had taken place and the terrible events of the previous year would act as a bedrock to teach me in practice at a level I had never previously been to. I trust that as you read on the insight I have gleaned will find rest in your heart and bring revelation to you. I can thank God that my experiences have led me to walk in a new dimension.

Chapter 3

FOUNDATIONS

Our re-instalment in Porth was obviously not popular with everyone and a few people left the church. We soon found that many people were hurting deeply due to their interpretation of events amongst the leaders! In short we had to know what it meant to love one another at God's **required** level. For years I had been seeking to understand the subject of keeping the Royal Law based on the Scripture found in: Matthew 22:37-20

In 1996 I had penned the following words believing them to be from God,

> *'The world has yet to see what can be achieved through a people that are fully committed to living out the Royal Law whilst at the same time embracing the full dynamics of the faith.'*

How I have longed to be a part of something like that – it is my dream. And we have begun to build this kind of church in Porth. I have learned that sin is not the obstacle to this revolutionary living, because it has been dealt with, rather the obstacle is self or the self-life. We must die in order that we can live! There are a number of obstacles, namely: sin, doubt, pride, self-life and fear, all of which can be devastating.

I knew that the fact that Jesus commanded us to love at his level meant that we should give it more thought than we did. I had previously pondered much on this; it was a subject that had niggled in my heart for years. I began to ask some questions of the Lord and he began to give me answers.

During my illness it seemed like my whole world had fallen apart, obviously my foundations had been flimsy in the hour of testing. It is easy to see that now but as previously stated, I was unable to think straight whilst under such duress. It is now obvious to me, that like most people, my faith had not been properly grounded or consolidated during my early years as a Christian. I have since learned that,

All the knowledge, understanding and experience gathered in life can only be absorbed into the foundation of what we are in essence. Right foundations, therefore, are imperative. The Scripture tells us that we must be <u>rooted</u> and <u>established</u> in love.

Coming to Christ gives us an opportunity to re-establish our foundations but sadly most Christians don't, and I was one who found it really difficult to accept myself and to understand that God doesn't stop loving us when we fail him.

We know that God is in covenant with us but do we fully understand what that means? In the book of Ephesians are recorded two prayers prayed by the apostle Paul. The latter is found in:

Ephesians 3:14-21

> *"For this reason I kneel before the Father, from whom his whole family in heaven and on earth derives its name. I pray that out of his glorious riches he may strengthen you with power through his Spirit in your inner being, so that Christ may dwell in your hearts through faith. And I pray that you being rooted and established in love, may have power together with all the saints, to grasp how wide and long and high and deep is the love of Christ, and to know this love that surpasses knowledge - that you may be filled to the measure of all the fullness of God. Now to him who is able to do immeasurably more than all we ask or imagine, according to his power that is at work within us, to him be glory in the church and in Christ Jesus throughout all generations, forever and ever! Amen."*

I knew full well that Christ dwells in our hearts through faith - but I didn't know that the more faith we have the more he dwells. Faith is **substance** even though it can't be seen. This means that faith is as real as the things that are seen. However, it is impossible to operate in this until you have understood what it is to be rooted and established in Love. When you think about it how can we?

"And I pray that you being rooted and established in love, may have power together with all the saints, to grasp how wide and long and high and deep is the love of Christ, and to know this love that surpasses knowledge - that you may be filled to the measure of all the fullness of God."

I want you to notice something here.

It is possible to be, *"filled to the measure of all the fullness of God."*

This measure is linked to our understanding and application of **loving at God's intended level.**

We are to be: *"rooted and established in love* **at God's intended level.***"* I cannot stress enough the highlighted part of the above statement.

Then we need to grasp: *"how wide and long and high and deep is the love of Christ, and to know this love that surpasses knowledge."* Furthermore, we need to grasp this when we come to Christ and not at some future date after the Devil has used our lack of knowledge against us. Be sure that our enemy Satan wants you to get used to Christianity at a much lower level than this.

In my own situation, I had been undone good and proper and the manner in which I was sinking should never happen to a child of God. I had been badly deceived by the evil one and it had worked a treat but now it seemed like I was daily learning new truths about building a proper foundation in Christ.

Sermons on this subject were coming fast and furious and in private counselling I was like a child with a new toy trying to show individuals what God had given me. In terms of my health there were good and bad days but now I had stopped interpreting the bad days as God's displeasure with me – this was an enormous breakthrough to bring me out of darkness. It is easy to write about this now that my mind has been transformed but I want you to know that if you are going through such a battle I really can empathise and if you apply what I am saying you will recover.

It is time to ask a question: is it really possible that, *"you may be filled to the measure of all the fullness of God."* Surely, if this be true then it is the answer to everything. Evangelism, non verbal and verbal would take care of itself. It dawned on me very clearly that we cannot continue to ignore God and then expect him to move among us and in our communities in Biblical proportions.

There is now no doubt in my mind that God has three priorities for our lives.

1) We are to love the Lord our God with all our hearts, souls, minds and strength.
2) We are to love our neighbour as we love ourselves.
3) We are to love one another as Christ has loved us.

These words are vitally important **with, as** and **as.**

We are to love the Lord our God (pause) with...
We are to love our neighbour (pause) as...
We are to love one another (pause) as...

This seems to be such simple teaching but I have been around long enough to know that we are missing it by a great distance!

The question is: Do we love according to the above clauses? That is, to love **no less** than at God's intended level?

All of the Law of the Prophets hang on these things. That means everything else is dependant on us understanding this truth and applying it to our lives. We think that we do love and we do, by this world's standards, but rarely are we loving at God's commanded level.

Please note that: we are dealing with commands here: these are not good ideas or requests. What can we expect from God if we ignore his commands? As someone who has served in the armed forces I fully understand that there are dire consequences in failing to obey a command.

At one particular time in my career in the Navy I had to be a part of a team in Northern Ireland who were trying to stop the gun-running activities of the IRA terrorists. It was a very dangerous job and not a pleasant six months of my life but I had no choice but to do it – I was under command.

One Sunday morning as I ministered in Porth God showed me clearly that we cannot do **that** *(perform miracles or bring to bear the power of God on a situation)* until we have done **this** *(loved at his commanded level)*. It was simple but it was clear.

I remember walking through a doorway to illustrate that there was a whole world of God's goodness and power through the door marked "Royal Law". I could see clearly that the goal of every Christian life should be to develop the character of Christ - this is why we should spend time with God, not so that we can bring him a shopping list of prayers but so that we can develop his nature and fulfil our obligation to keep the Royal Law. If we walk through the door marked "Royal law" we will find another door marked "Revelation Knowledge". And this latter door will be opened to us in its uncorrupted state.

I was beginning to see that for the past few months I had

been living through the first part of Psalm 23, *"The Lord is my shepherd I shall not want, he makes me to lie down in green pastures, he leads me by quiet waters, he restores my soul. He causes me to walk on paths of righteousness for his names sake."*

In the midst of him making, causing and leading, he is restoring. It had been a hard nightmarish journey but I am now writing what you are reading.

He wants to *restore your soul* too. When? Well, right now! As near to the beginning of your Christian walk as possible. Don't waste another day! Today and not later, you should learn who you are in Christ! *"Be transformed by the renewing of your mind."* Romans 12:3

If we are to love God, *with all of our strength* - then we must be restored into his image.

> *a)* **We must have a changed** *heart.*
> *b)* **We must have a renewed** *mind.*
> *c)* **We must have a restored** *soul.*

Then we can love him with all our **strength** because we are not wasting energy in a needless direction.

That's why: He makes, causes, and leads.

He makes me to lie down in green pastures, He leads me by quiet waters, He causes me to walk on paths of righteousness for his names sake.

Has God led you into the situation you find yourself in today? No… you cry he couldn't possibly, it is so horrible. Well yes… but you must understand that God does everything from an eternal perspective. The situation I found myself in was a nightmare but much of the defeat that I felt inside could have been avoided if I had been rooted and established in his love. You see, my worst fears, during the illness, was that God had given up on me, even to the point that I was now going to hell.

Have you ever felt that you have blown it completely or that you have committed the unpardonable sin? If so you are not alone – certainly not alone! Indeed you are in good company but the fact is you have yet to understand God's amazing grace which means the greater the sin the greater the grace.

For me it wasn't that I thought I had committed the unpardonable sin but my inability to rationalise God's hand on me when I was in such a state. The truth is, you will never be able to adequately love others until you have realised how much grace is available to you, yourself.

No doubt, like me, you have a problem of interpreting God through how you feel or the circumstances that you find yourself in. Consequently, the enemy will find it easy to tilt you off balance. You are more secure than you think my dear friend! You see it is not so much what happens to us along life's journey it is more important how we interpret what happens to us along life's journey.

And we will interpret these happenings according to the foundation that we are looking out from. Can we ask: what can I learn from this in order that I can mature? I learned a long time ago that God is more concerned with our maturity than he is with our temporal happiness. Happiness is a state we will experience forever. For now however, we can expect a few blips but even during the blips God, our Father, is never far away, he is:

"an ever present help in times of trouble." Psalm 46:1

And in James 1:3-4 we are encouraged by the following:

"Consider it pure joy whenever you face trials of many kinds because the testing of your faith develops perseverance and perseverance must finish its work so that you are mature and complete not lacking in anything."

It is imperative that you know that God wants all of his children to be in this state, *"not lacking in anything"*. This state is only achieved as we meet God's conditions but these conditions are not to be a futile attempt to keep the law. No, the law has been made obsolete for the child of God. You are free but if you want to lack nothing then you have an obligation and that is to, *"Walk in the Spirit"* and this is achieved when we love at God's intended level.

If this becomes the goal of our lives then we will be both fulfilled and effective for God. We have to realise that he expects us to work at this and holds us responsible because it does not come naturally and needs determined cultivation. I had wanted this state for years but there were so many weaknesses in the area of my soul that it was impossible. How can you walk in love at this level when you won't believe that God loves **you** at this level? You can only possibly give eternal love to the degree that you have allowed yourself to receive it. You should be looking up far more than you are looking down; you should be smiling much more than you are – how Satan wants to fill your mind with negatives!

God dwells in the believer's heart so the key to life is allowing Jesus to be released from within. This is what had happened in that extraordinary meeting at the Elim conference in 2000. One of the biggest mistakes we have made is not seeing the seriousness of consolidating new believers. Until we are rooted and established in love we will be limited because we can only do **that** (*with all that that entails*) when we have understood **this.**

Are we too busy trying to find out things that we are not sure of to the degree that we are ignoring the things that are obvious? Could it be that God is saying, 'I am not telling you anything else until you do what I have already told you?'

"Seek first the kingdom of God and his righteousness and all these things shall be added to you." Matthew 6:33

One thing that is clear in the word of God is, God didn't say, "seek first the church"! He said, *"Seek first the Kingdom..."* The church is part of seeking the kingdom but while we can exhaust all that the church is, we can never exhaust the kingdom. The fact is we either listen to the word of God or we hear other voices the mind is not neutral. We have a choice but due to neglect most of us are listening to voices other than the word of God.

However, it is clear,
> *"man does not live on bread alone but on every word that proceeds from the mouth of God."* Matthew 4:4

We gain further instruction on this in:

> Proverbs 4:20-21, *"My son pay attention to what I say; listen closely to my words. Do not let them out of your sight, keep them within your heart; for they are life to those who find them and health to a man's whole body. Above all else guard your heart for it is the wellspring of life."*

King David was chosen because of the condition of his heart. Satan's attempt is to harden your heart so that he can stop you at source by nullifying the wellspring of life. Has he succeeded? The seed of life that God places within us is both creative and unending. Faith based on love means that nothing is impossible for those who believe. Satan is well aware of that fact so he does his utmost to spoil it by hardening our hearts – the heart is hardened whenever we walk in unforgiveness, bitterness, lack of love etc.

We have access to supernatural provision and the means of this provision is faith but you can't understand that until you have understood that you will not walk in revelation knowledge unless you are loving at God's intended level.

The doorway then to supernatural provision is to keep the Royal Law.

Have you ever wondered why God doesn't just appear to his followers? Well the answer is we can achieve more by understanding and applying faith than we could by seeing God. Faith is the outworking of revelation knowledge which is far superior to knowledge that comes to us through the senses. The Lord does not often appear because his appearance would be interpreted by the senses whereas his word is interpreted by revelation knowledge. Faith is more powerful than sight - we have not fully understood what can be achieved by faith. We pass through the doorway into another realm by loving at **God's intended level** and through that door is all that we need provided by the spirit realm. It is an exciting place and is obtainable to all believers.

"The only thing that counts is faith expressing itself through love." Galatians 6:9

The Bible clearly speaks about a realm where believers can dwell where we can achieve incredible things by faith, a place where we have authority over the evil one. It is a place of supernatural provision where heavenly gifts are sent by God.

The problem is you can't have that until you have done this!

Until we are rooted and established in "This Love" you can't pass through the door where the realm of the spirit is a manifest, continuous reality. But once you have sought to keep God's commandments on love he removes the partitioning wall. Faith is not a product of the reasoning faculties but rather of the re-created spirit. Faith can only be received from another world. Once we are certain that we have God's word on a situation we can speak it into being:

"You shall say to this mountain..."

The problem is most believers unnecessarily remain at the wrong side of the partitioning wall because we try to do this before we have done that. Can you understand? So often we make no real attempt to keep the Royal Law but try to walk in positive confession in order to activate the promises of God. Now you know why we remain relatively powerless!

Listen! God is not a liar. His word is true but there is a reason why we are not experiencing it in its fullness.

Let's face it, we have been sold an untruth that trying to cast out devils, heal the sick, devise plans to reach the lost or soak in the Spirit *(all valid things)* is more exciting than it is to work at loving at God's required level. We must adopt normal Biblical practices that result in supernatural consequence. Don't live for one moment longer under the wrong perspective – God has provided everything we need for both maintenance and growth. He is still able to create on our behalf.

Make no mistake, it is God's intention that we can come to a place in him where we can speak to situations and change them. God is saying to you, 'If you will love at my required level then you will also do all that is promised in my word.'

Severe harm can be done in an instant and all that is needed is a tongue. Severe good usually takes longer until we realise that we have authority to break Satan's power in a person's life by using our tongues alone!

These truths were helping me to lay a new foundation in my own life and also amongst the congregation at Porth –

never had I felt so hopeful; never had my heart been so full of faith; never had I felt that I was more than a conqueror than I was beginning to feel. Life for me, and others, was taking on new dimensions as God was revealing to me the secret things of the kingdom. I was moving from what I thought was death into life.

Chapter 4

BEGINNINGS

Through vast amounts of personal study and a variety of experiences I have concluded that the most important thing in our dealings with God is how something begins.

We can safely say that if something begins in God it will definitely end well. With this in mind I am very concerned that most Christians are not given the benefit of beginning well. As long as you have a good beginning, a solid grounding in who God is *(an unwavering knowledge of his nature)* and who you are in him – you will have no problem applying the following.

> *"We live by faith and not by sight."* 2 Corinthians 5:7

> *"So we fix our eyes not on what is seen but what is unseen for what is seen is temporary but what is unseen is eternal."* 2 Corinthians 4:18

Remember: that in terms of Kingdom principles,' If you can see it - it's not permanent'. The same is true of touch, sight, smell and hearing. In other words if it is communicated to you by the senses it has no permanence. The things that are unseen are communicated to us through Spirit.

It is the Spirit in a man that brings understanding.

Take heart in the following words.

> **"He who began a good work in you will complete it until the Day of Jesus Christ."** Philippians 1:6

If God begins something we can guarantee that God will complete it.

The biggest question therefore is, whether or not something has its origins in God or not. In other words did God begin it? All that we have to do is to find the beginning and to make sure that that beginning is in God. It follows then that all that you need from God has a beginning point.

The principle of this is found in Genesis chapter one:

> *"In the beginning God."*

And also in John 1:1

"In the beginning was the word and the word was with God and the word was God."

Because God began it God will finish it. In the book of Hebrews we read of the great heroes of Faith,

> Hebrews 11:13, *"All these people were still living by faith when they died. They did not receive the things promised; they only saw them and welcomed them from a distance."*

"From a distance..."

Faith will look into the distance. We must look beyond natural horizons...as long as you have walked through the door you will start to see what is beyond the door. As we shall establish, faith does not come through seeing - it comes through hearing. We are called to see beyond what we see in the natural sense. And this kind of seeing does not actually come through seeing but rather through hearing. I cannot say for sure when I found my beginning point that led me to be healed but I did find one and that's the important thing.

In Romans 10:17 we are told:

> *"Faith comes by hearing and hearing by the word of God."*

And in Galatians 3:5

"Does God give you his spirit and work miracles among you because you obey the law or because you believe what you heard?"

Faith is not faith unless its source is the voice of God speaking either in general terms or specific terms. So, if we are sick we must determine what God is saying to us about the illness. If we have financial problems we must hear what God is saying about it. We must hear and apply what he says about marriage, child rearing and apply it and so on and so forth.

I have been using the term **beginning point** repeatedly because it is absolutely vital. Again I want to stress again its importance because if you can find that beginning point in God then the outcome is assured even if the answer is still in the distance - it will eventually draw near. We are assured of this because it is a universal law in God that **if he commences, he also concludes.**

Read that again – several times if necessary until you have digested it.

Sometimes we can't perceive a good outcome because we know we haven't got the resources to achieve it. What we should do is seize the chance that God gives us and submit ourselves to his discipleship and he will provide the resources.

Every beginning in God has an end result that is favourable in God. That is why God can reassure us that,

> *"All things work out together for the good for those who love the Lord."* Romans 8:28.

Your part is in the loving - cultivating the essential part of your relationship with God. We should all have the following beginning point in terms of our relationship with God which leads into our service for God.

> *"Therefore, I urge you brothers in view of God's mercy to offer your bodies as living sacrifices holy and pleasing to God. This is your spiritual act of worship. Do not conform any longer to the pattern of this world but be transformed by the renewing of your mind. THEN you will be able to test and approve what God's will is - his good, pleasing and perfect will for your life."*
> Romans 12:1-4

The same passage of Scripture taken from The Message, reads,

> *"So here's what I want you to do, God helping you: take your everyday, ordinary life - your sleeping, eating, going-to-work and walking around life - and place it before God as an offering. Embracing what*

God does for you is the best thing you can do for him. Don't become so well-adjusted to your culture that you fit into it without even thinking. Instead fix your attention on God. You'll be changed from the inside out. Readily recognize what he wants from you, and quickly respond to it. Unlike the culture around you, always dragging you down to its level of immaturity, God brings the best out of you, develops well-formed maturity in you."

We need to give thought to the word THEN!

How long should the new convert give into digesting and understanding the importance of this? The fact that it is easily bypassed is in large part a reason why we find ourselves so impotent.

The promises of God are all in existence on your behalf. But they will remain distant until we meet the conditions which release the keys of the kingdom and bring the promises of God into our possession.

Faithfulness without the ongoing obedience to God's directing is not enough. Faithfulness accompanied by obedience is what God is looking for.

We should be left in no doubt: Faith leading to obedience is the key that opens the windows of heaven to release the blessings of heaven into the earth's atmosphere.

What parameters and horizons have we imposed upon ourselves? God wants us to see beyond those parameters and horizons. And if you have lost your way you need to find a new beginning. All that you have to do is to find a beginning point and allow God to stretch you. I found one and it has projected me into a realm I had not previously experienced – without doubt, you can too!

Maybe your traditions or past experiences have imposed limitations on what you can believe God for. Well, perhaps it is time to ask: why you are so limited.

We should ask more questions of what we have accepted. You are more than you have become.

Why do we do what we do?

Why do we see it that way?

Why do we impose such limitations on ourselves?

In answering these questions begin again. Find your beginning point in God.

How?

Do whatever is necessary to hear his voice for your situation. Maybe you need to go back to the point where you allowed a stumbling block to come into your life. Start today...either way you need a spiritual answer. A new foundation can begin this very minute if you will talk with God from an open heart.

Here is a solid Biblical prayer to help you:

> *"Search me O God and know my heart test me and know my anxious thoughts."* Psalm 139:23

I repeat: all the knowledge and understanding that we glean can only be absorbed into the foundation of what we are in essence. Foundations therefore are imperative!

Dig some new ones today. I did and it has and is continuing to transform my life. Don't accept the status quo – it is not final.

Whoever you are and whatever you have done you can change and change is accomplished by one major decision followed by a series of choices.

It is high time that we developed a new norm in the church of Jesus Christ.

We can still write the next chapter in determining the legacy we shall leave those who follow us. With all the resources of heaven that are available to us may we decide conclusively to do so?

Chapter 5

THE SECRET OF ANOINTED SERVICE

We must develop love by making faith decisions because we will all have many tangible reasons not to love at God's intended level. For example: it takes faith to leave justice to God rather than to desire revenge. It takes faith to love the unlovely. It takes faith to give precious time and money into the Kingdom of God that in the natural we can ill afford to give.

The Apostle Paul said in Philippians 3:3,

> *"I place no confidence in the flesh."* and in Ephesians 6:10 *"Be strong in the Lord and in his mighty power."*

Folks, we must go beyond the flesh. During my illness the day came where I realised beyond any shadow of doubt that I simply had to go beyond what I was seeing, feeling and imagining. Most importantly imagining! Actively cast down your imaginations. Don't wait until they go away

At all times we can rely on God's presence and strength at our time of need. And I believe it will be manifest to us in the area that we need it most. "When we are weak, then he is strong." And as the songwriter said, 'Now let the weak say I am strong.' Love has its greatest effect when it flows through human weakness. We are involved in God's work and he is always strong! Death is only an enemy when a person's soul feels insecure. Otherwise it is most certainly a promotion.

Therefore, our main task is to find out what pleases him and do it. We can be certain that the main way to please God is to fulfil the greatest command, to strive to love him with all of our hearts, soul, mind and strength and then to love **for him** by loving our neighbour as we love ourselves. If we can become filled to all the fullness of God and then learn to release that life then God will surely do more than we can ask, hope or imagine. Listen: hear me now, as long as God's life is released he will do more than we can ask, hope or imagine and the glory goes to him.

There is a vast difference between anointing and hype but from the naked eye they can look the same. The key to releasing the life of God from within is to understand the following: Jesus passes out of our beings into the atmosphere through the heart. However, the trapdoor of the heart *(so to speak)* can only be opened from the inside, in other words by him. It is not by human strength or by education or by hyping up a meeting it is by loving at his level and determining right motives for service. Then at the right time he will come...

I repeat: King David's strength was not in his sword or his muscles it was in the condition of his heart!

Christian life is not about position or even location it is about him - our ongoing relationship with him. When that is in place he will give the opportunities on a daily basis. Above all, get rooted and established in love. Work at it - set goals, give time, energy and resources to it. Make the goal of your life to be the development of the character of Christ. Be restored into the image of God and in so doing you will definitely reconcile people back to God and play a part in restoring them into the image of God.

Remember the following pattern:

We change our hearts.

Renew our minds.

Restore our souls.

What stage are you at today?

Even though I had been a Christian for 16 years including serving God as a pastor and missionary I realise now that I had not understood this most essential of Christian doctrines. The reality that, **FAITH EQUALS RIGHTEOUSNESS**

It is not performance that leads to righteousness it is faith. Oh what a revelation. If you have faith in Christ then despite lapses in your behaviour you are righteous before God. No wonder we have called this Amazing Grace!

> *"Abraham believed God and it was credited to him as righteousness."*
> Romans 4:6-8

David says the same thing when he speaks of the blessedness of the man to whom God credits righteousness apart from works:

Psalm 32:1-2 says,

> *"Blessed are they whose transgressions are forgiven, whose sins are covered. Blessed is the man whose sin the Lord will never count against him."*

NEVER! - The reason that our sins are not **counted** against us is because righteousness has been **credited** to us. If faith equates to righteousness, then how does it equate to the rest of the package of the gospel? Think on this for a moment: if we receive eternity by believing *(only)*; then surely **all things** are received by believing - that is through faith! Satan is warring against this revelation and in my case he had almost won the battle. More than I needed the medical profession *(and I did)* I needed an injection of faith. There is no doctor on earth who can heal a spiritual problem through medicine alone.

> *"Now faith is being sure of what we hope for and certain of what we do not see. This is what the ancients were commended for."* *And without faith it is impossible to please God, because anyone who comes to him must believe that he exists and that he rewards those who earnestly seek him."* Hebrews 11:1

Faith believes the impossible!

Remember that faith is not a product of the reasoning faculties but of the recreated spirit! There are two kinds of knowledge - sense knowledge and revelation knowledge. Since January 2001 I had been forced to find this out my survival and the welfare of my family depended on it. The issue ceased to be merely a theological topic.

Faith has to believe back before it can believe forward.

> *"By faith we understand that the universe was formed at God's command, so that what is seen was not made out of what was visible."* Hebrews 11:3

"By faith he (Abraham) left Egypt, not fearing the king's anger; he persevered because he saw him who is invisible." Hebrews 11:27

"The only thing that counts is faith expressing itself through love." Galatians 6:9

You have to believe what God has done in the past before you can believe God for the future. Likewise there are times when you have to look back to what God has already said to you.

Faith is believing and not a feeling. Faith is seeing the invisible because the word of God declares it to be true. We must look at life through the grid of scripture. What a place there is to come to in Him...God asks us to believe back at a personal level as well to what he has said about us,. For example:

"Reckon yourself dead to sin..." Romans 6:11

"You died to sin so how can you live in it any longer." Romans 6:7

"Without faith it is impossible to please God." Hebrews 11:6

"This is the work of God to believe in the one he sent and to love one another has he commanded us." 1 John 3:23

"You are more than a conqueror." Romans 8:37

We must believe what God has said! I struggled to believe God particularly in relation to what God's word has to say positively about me. That is why I needed to be rooted and established in love at God's level. I needed to see the extent in which God loved me. God makes it clear in his word just how much he loves us and the same is true regarding health and well being. If we don't understand just how much God loves us then we will be fodder for the enemy because he will always convince us that we are experiencing evil because we have let God down. Be warned because this battle worsens for those who are seeking to be, *"Pure in heart"*. Sin, law and perceived judgment will come to us hand-in-hand.

So if we are to receive healing in the present; we must look back to what God has said in the past:

"He took up our sickness and our infirmities and by His stripes we are healed." Matthew 8:17

"Abraham believed God and it was credited to him as righteousness."
Romans 4:3

Can you begin to see this as a pattern?

If we believe what God says about healing will healing be **credited** to us?

It is clear from Scripture that God looks for Faith more than for moral perfection. The promises of God are activated in our lives when we look at the three things that remain.

"Now these three things remain faith, hope and love." 1 Corinthians 13:13

We believe and obey God's commands to **love** at His level. This foundation fills our hearts with **hope** that we can receive the promises of God by **Faith.** Your confidence lifts immensely when you know that God knows it is your desire and practice to keep the Royal Law found in Scripture.

Faith is something we do - we must reason if you have said this then I will do it. Love is something we do! It is imperative to know that we really must discipline ourselves to both hear and speak the language of faith which is in reality a subsidiary of the language of love.

We have a responsibility; an obligation. If you continually want to receive by faith then you must walk in the Spirit. This means that you must do whatever is necessary for you to walk in the Spirit. As this revelation took root in my heart my confidence began to grow and I started to sleep like a baby in fact better than I've ever done. I was still feeling weakness in my heart at times and went back to Manchester for a routine consultation. Strangely, as the day approached the worse I began to feel and as I sat in my consultant's office I felt fairly low. Mr. Bennet my consultant entered reading my notes as he slowly walked through the office, 'Hmm you have been through a pretty difficult time' he murmured and then paused before continuing with something totally unexpected, 'well, I won't need to see you again because you are cured.'

I didn't feel cured but I thanked him and left feeling that somehow God had spoken that day. Even though Mr. Bennet was not speaking to me out of a spiritual perspective I received those words by faith and took them to heart and now in the time that has passed since I'm glad to say I have not needed to see him again. In fact as I write I am very sportingly active again, jogging, swimming, playing badminton…all things I never thought I would do again. In fact I have recently completed a seven mile run the furthest I have run for several years. If we can hear from God and then see it in the spirit we **will** eventually do it.

What riches are ahead for those who will learn to, *"Walk in the Spirit."*

> Galatians 5:16, *"So I say, live by the Spirit, and you will not gratify the desires of the sinful nature. For the sinful nature desires what is contrary to the Spirit and the Spirit what is contrary to the sinful nature. They are in conflict with each other, so that you do not do what you want. But if you are led by the Spirit, you are not under law."*

What does it mean by, *"you are not be under the Law?"*

Well the Scripture tells us that, *"He who loves his fellow man has fulfilled the Law."*

This is true because of Jesus words in Matthew 22:37-40,

> *"Love the LORD your God with all of your heart, with all of your soul and with all of your mind. This is the first and greatest commandment. And the second is like it; love your neighbour as yourself. All the law and the prophets hang on these two commandments."*

Again we need to stress that this love is no ordinary love, it is love that enters our world from another world. It is nothing less than the character and nature of a God of love flowing from the essence of his being. God has poured this love into our hearts in order that we in turn can pour it out of our hearts. It is a love that destroys our enemies by making them our friends. A love that would rather be wronged than seek revenge, a love that delights to give grace, mercy, forgiveness and possessions even when it is not merited. It is love that does not treat us or others as our sin deserves. It is the first and greatest command and also the greatest need of the church.

Every decision and action should be made from the foundation of **this love** because "God is love." This love far exceeds all other attempts at love because it is the only level of love that places no conditions. This is how we know what love is: *"Jesus Christ laid down his life for us and we ought to lay down our lives for our brothers"* 1 John 3:16

It is fair to say, wherever God's love flows, God's presence abides. The Great Commission relies on God's church to live out the Great Commandment! On from this we need to understand that it is no use setting goals for the Great Commission if we will not do so out of the foundation of the Great Commandment.

Most things that we do can be imitated but not this - it is impossible to imitate love at God's intended level and this is surely the point of the command. Jesus himself alluded to the fact that the way we love one another is the ingredient by which men would know that his disciples belonged to him.

The decision to walk in this love is far more powerful than receiving a miracle of healing because it will turn an otherwise selfish person into a self-less person. What a witness such a person becomes!

> *"Love covers over a multitude of sins."* 1 Peter 4:8

> *"Love never fails."* 1 Corinthians 13:8

> *"Now these three remain faith, hope and love."* 1 Corinthians 13:13

Behold a great truth; the Great Commission must be fulfilled out of the Great Command!

How difficult it is for us to understand that God will not accept anything less from us than the fulfilling of his commands to love. Because we have, in the main, offered far less to him we do not realise what we have denied ourselves and others. It is time to prove life at this level. What will God do in response to our fulfillment of his commands? The answer is more than we can hope ask or imagine! That is he will turn up and do all the things that we have been trying to do in our own strength. True maturity is measured by our ability to love unconditionally. This is the revolution that God is seeking-this in turn will turn our community upside down. It will!

"Do not judge and you will not be judged, do not condemn and you will not be condemned. Forgive and you will be forgiven. Give and it will be given to you. A good measure pressed down, shaken together and running over, will be poured into your lap. For with the measure you use it will be measured to you." Luke 6:37

Often this Scripture is quoted in relation to money but it goes much further than money. It says, you will be judged to the same measure that you judge others and condemned to the same degree that you are condemning others. Are you judging? Are you condemning? If you are don't try and justify it, because it is self defeating, like taking poison and waiting for the other person to die. However, if you have to forgive big sins committed against you God will forgive your big sins. So do you need to forgive anybody some big sins? If you do, then store up some mercy credit in your own account by going ahead and forgiving.

Don't Judge! Don't Condemn! **Do** forgive! It is so clear as to be obvious but repeatedly we cannot keep God's word and, at worst, we choose to ignore it.

The Apostle Paul said,

"The only thing that counts is faith expressing itself through love." Galatians 6:9

We have a problem because we all justify our condemnation and judgment of other believers. Forgiveness and acceptance are total in God's economy. The goal of our lives and the stress upon our wills should be that we **"love one another as he has loved us."** I have certainly not lived this out to the degree that the Lord wants me to but I do believe in it with all of my heart and hopefully, I am pressing on toward this.

This kind of love is lived out of the will and not the feelings - we are called to do it regardless of how we may feel. Sure it will be tested but there is a never ending fountain of God's grace so that we can indeed find God's strength in the midst of our trials. If you want to forgive – you can forgive because it is a supernatural thing.

> John 3:14 **"We know that we have passed from death to life because we love our brothers. Anyone who does not love remains in death."**

Unconditional love is the greatest power in the universe. At the scene of the crucifixion it caused an earthquake, people to come out of their graves and an inanimate object to tear. Yet, we are usually so poor at living out this side of Christian life that we have no proof of life in this direction. Are we expecting God to move in power when we will not forgive people for far less than God has had to forgive us for?

We owe a debt of love at this level.

"Let no debt remain outstanding except the continuing debt to love." Romans 13:8

Listen for the voice of the Lord: **"Above all, love one another."**

Without any shadow of doubt LOVE equates to POWER!

At any moment we are only a decision away from this kind of love. Our general inability to understand this subject has cost us more than we can imagine. For me it has been a personal journey over many years. As I took up pastoral ministry again in Porth, I was determined to lay again a new foundation. After all I had suffered this lack of unconditional love in Porth, seen others suffer and no doubt made others suffer; the same can be said of my time in Africa and would, of course, be repeated in any situation. This time I had come amongst a hurting people. I continued to speak of, 'love at God's intended level' in practically every sermon and gradually one by one I could sense that people were being healed in their hearts. For some this was taking longer than others and it is true to say that there are minorities who are still hurting but those who have lived through this will testify that it has taken place. God is true to his word!

As I write this part of the book I am overlooking the beautiful – afore mentioned - Oxwich Bay, on South Wales'

Gower Peninsular. I have had an interesting day attending an evangelism seminar with the Elim church. Later I called in at the Bible College of Wales – the place built by faith by Rhys Howells. It was good to breathe in the atmosphere of the college and all that it has stood for over the years. Today, however, it is a pale shadow of its former glory attracting just a few students. Like many of the great and renowned evangelic sites that survive in Wales, without God's hand in the present day it may well become a museum piece – though I quickly add, may God forbid this!

As I later walked through the village at Oxwich I saw a plaque on a cottage proclaiming that John Wesley had stayed in the cottage and preached five times from there over the years. I imagined this legend of a man traveling for hours on horseback to what must have seemed such a remote place to him to deposit the gospel in the hearts of his listeners. What a heritage! One is reminded of the tremendous role that Christianity has played in forming all that is great in Wales. Why then is the British nation so indifferent today? What would have happened if the teaching of the Royal Law had been paramount rather than the oft mentioned religious bigotry and pride that overwhelmed the populace, particularly since the great Welsh revival in 1904?

The revival began in Moriah chapel Loughor and is still revered throughout the evangelical world and remains a place of pilgrimage for many. Nevertheless, many of the inhabitants of Loughor today have no idea where Moriah chapel is, let alone its significance.

I had given this prophecy in 1995 during an Evangelistic crusade with Marilyn Harry in Ynyshir, Rhondda.

'God will not revive his church in Wales if we remain apathetic and if we will not pursue holiness. Revival will remain but a dream if we will not allow God into our comfort zones to stir us up and cause us to will revival. We must realise that by and large we have moved far from real, Biblical Christianity. God is calling us back to the simplicity of a pursuit of holy living and a willingness to obey him no matter what the cost. God is taking us out of our comfort zones and into the adventure of action packed, risk taking obedience to his voice. We must adopt God centered living and build churches that reflect God rather than having people at the center of their function and mandates. In this day of reckoning will anyone pay the price that will bring revival? Can God gather enough sufficiently dead-to-self people to fill the pulpits of our land, so that his voice can truly speak and not be watered down? Can enough people be gathered to forsake all, in order to impact Wales at a national level? Will enough gather to share the burden, weep the tears and pray the prayers to reverse our fall from grace? The word of the Lord is: Set the trumpet to your mouths, hearken and speak my words rather than platitudes of what people's itching hears want to hear.

Speak my words! Speak my words! For my words will surely be accompanied by my power.'

I also gave the following prophetic word in Porth in 2001

Set the trumpet to your mouth and call back all the wounded and defeated sheep, for I will turn them into an army that will sweep this land. Many are waiting to hear that they have another chance and my grace is sufficient; many of these sheep have been abused through leadership and hurt by my body which has acted through lack of knowledge and lack of wisdom.

I believe that we should acknowledge that we have not kept the Royal Law and follow our acknowledgement by repenting. If we do we can then set about creating a new norm that will be in place for future generations. We have been outsmarted by the enemy by closing the door named Royal Law. Maybe due to this we have faced needless death in the truest sense of the word. But in the Bible death never means cessation of life - it always means separation. To be disconnected from God is spiritual death. Physical death is separation from the body. All new life comes through death, burial and resurrection. If I can know him in the power of his suffering I can know him in his resurrection. Expect to face some little deaths. You are perpetually going through a cycle of death, burial and resurrection that is normal Christian living but what you thought would happen, during the death period, hasn't happened. Jesus is always on time!

Remember the grain of wheat principle. In Christianity death leads to multiplication. Normal activity leads to addition but it is death that leads to multiplication. Death is separation! Listen, death is separation! That is why there are times when you will not feel God's presence. But you must have the following attitude, 'I'm coming up out of it.

> *"No weapon forged against you will prevail."* Isaiah 54:17

When the veil was TORN from the top down God was demonstrating more than just his power – he was demonstrating his intent.

Jesus saw the heavens tear. If necessary, God will tear up heaven to get you out of the problem you are facing. The answer is written in the sky! During our visit back to the UK before my illness I was preaching in Treorchy in the Rhondda Valleys. On the afternoon preceding the evening meeting I was praying with my friend Andrew Smith *(one of the Elders at Porth)*, when I prophesied those words, 'The Answer is written in the sky.' At the time that I prophesied it I had no idea what it meant or of the relevance that it would have upon my faith.

One day after my return to the Rhondda I felt God ask me, 'what did I think was beyond the stars'. Quite by chance I did a bit of amateur astronomy. There is so much out there beyond what we can see – even with a telescope, but heaven must be torn in order for you to see it.

The Bible says,

*"He who descended has also ascended to fill
the whole Universe."* Ephesians 4:10

We must pray in authority at the same time as keeping the Royal Law until we create an open heaven because when the heavens are torn open we shall see a mirror image of the life of God as it should be lived and worked out in his presence. Death is a wonderful thing if you deal with it properly! It is merely temporal separation from what you have known.

We are not too perturbed if we are out-sung by the crowds in the rock world; not too dismayed if we are out given by the charities; not too down hearted if our building projects are not recognised but we should be absolutely tortured if we are out loved by any group on this earth. God is love!

It is not enough to recognise God through the miraculous acts we perform - other people can perform miraculous acts. We will only truly be recognised by the extent of our love!

We cannot interpret the things surrounding God, His church and His people through natural means. Most believers who are not spiritually aware do just that. The first question that we need to ask is, what is God doing in this and, secondly, what will be achieved, for God, in this?

The question of authority has been settled once and for all – God won and Satan lost. The problem is we have ignored God's blue-print on how to effect the victory. Oh how blind we have been – we would rather shout at a dodging target than love our neighbour.

If only we can grasp the amount of grace that has been apportioned to us and then respond in love we would accordingly begin to move mountains.

Chapter 6

BY THE WAY OF THE CROSS

So often our natural response to revelation of the true gospel according to God's amazing grace is: 'this is too good to be true,'

"What shall we say, then? Shall we go on sinning so that grace may increase? By no means! We died to sin; how can we live in it any longer? Or don't you know that all of us who were baptized into Christ Jesus were baptized into his death? We were therefore buried with him through baptism into death in order that, just as Christ was raised from the dead through the glory of the Father, we too may live a new life. If we have been united with him like this in his death, we will certainly also be united with him in his resurrection. For we know that our old self was crucified with him so that the body of sin might be done away with, that we

should no longer be slaves to sin— because anyone who has died has been freed from sin. Romans 6:6-8

I have come by the way of the cross. If you truly come by the way of the Cross then you have been crucified with Christ and you no longer live but Christ lives in you. This has happened – past tense.

You do not have to keep crucifying yourself. In fact you can't – you simply have to reckon yourself dead or realise that it has happened past tense – once and for all. The battle in the mind goes like this: 'how can you be crucified when you still think that way and still do the sinning that you do?' I shall seek to answer this.

You have been crucified but if you have been baptised you have been resurrected.This has already taken place...The fact that you are still very much alive does not negate the fact that you have died. I used to think that when the Apostle Paul wrote,

> *"I have been crucified with Christ and I no longer live but Christ lives in me, the life I live in the body I live by faith in the Son of God who died and gave himself for me,"* Galatians 2:22

that he had achieved something that few believers achieve.

One day, however, God revealed to me that this is the state of all born again believers we just don't realise it or reckon it to be true.

> *"Now if we died with Christ, we believe that we will also live with him. For we know that since Christ was raised from the dead, he cannot die again; death no longer has mastery over him. The death he died, he died to sin once for all; but the life he lives, he lives to God. In the same way, count (reckon) yourselves dead to sin but alive to God in Christ Jesus. Therefore do not let sin reign in your mortal body so that you obey its evil desires. Do not offer the parts of your body to sin, as instruments of wickedness, but rather offer yourselves to God, as those who have been brought from death to life; and offer the parts of your body to him as instruments of righteousness. For sin shall not be your master, because you are not under law, but under grace."* Romans 6:8-14

> *"Reckon yourself dead to sin but alive to God in Christ Jesus."*

Don't stand at the crossroads - decide to be a kingdom person. Don't waver any longer at the crossroads of indecision – 'reckon!'

The Kingdom of God bares absolutely no resemblance to this world. None at all! We live in a parallel universe. One part is governed by the senses the other is governed by the Spirit. One is fuelled by sense knowledge; one is fuelled by revelation knowledge.

In and through us the one should bring the other into submission. The Spirit is superior – far superior. Once we realise this then we will run to God, we will hunger and thirst after God. We will do anything to bring heaven's blessing into the world's atmosphere.

Sense knowledge is governed by seeing. Revelation knowledge is governed by hearing. Some of us can't hear because we are dominated by what we see.

People can become a blockage because God sees what they will be whereby we see only what they are or perversely what they are not! Stop letting your faith be dominated by sight and start letting it be dominated by what you hear.
Listen and hear: *"Faith comes by hearing and hearing by the word of God."*

Because we have not yet seen we struggle to believe what we have heard. But we are working to God's timescale and not him to ours. We often disqualify ourselves because we lift revelation from the heart and store it in the mind. We move from revelation knowledge and rely again on sense knowledge.

"So we live by faith and not by sight." 2 *Corinthians 5:7*

"We fix our eyes not on what is seen but what is unseen for what is seen is temporary but what is unseen is eternal" **UNSEEN** 2 *Corinthians 4:18*

Faith comes by hearing because the hearing takes you beyond your seen horizons. You have subconsciously imposed boundaries, barriers and limitations on your life.

Undo the lie today and begin to hear what the Bible says about you. Then take the step of faith through the doorway and into life in the kingdom of God.

As we have seen, in simple terms, the kingdom of God means: 'If you will do **this** then I will do **that**.'

You must unlearn the way that you have learned in the past. Come out of your prison and begin to live at God's level. Live a parallel life. Live by kingdom principles! Live by kingdom principles! We must stop seeing this as a negative – it is absolutely positive.

Would you rather be a **nobody** and gain the benefits of the kingdom or be a **somebody** in the eyes of the world and not gain the benefits of the kingdom.

As we have seen, sin and law walk toward you hand in

hand - the sin to trap you the Law to make you feel condemned. This is swiftly followed by deceitful judgement – the devils attempt to convince you of a lie concerning your future. So God says the Law is no longer in affect in the life of the believer. It is once and for all abolished… because it has fully served its purpose in evangelising you. You have so much worth that the purpose of the Law was to evangelise you. Can you see it? We have believed a lie – a lie that tells us that God expected us to keep the Law. Learn today God does not expect you to keep the Law.

Marvel at the following Scriptures: Galatians 3:10-14, *"All who rely on observing the Law are under a curse, for it is written, 'Cursed is everyone who does not continue to do everything written in the book of the Law.' Clearly no one is justified before God by the Law, because, The Righteous will live by faith. The Law is not based on faith, on the contrary, the man who does these things will live by them. Christ redeemed us from the curse of the Law by becoming a curse for us, for it is written. 'Cursed is everyone who is hung on a tree.' He redeemed us in order that the blessing given to Abraham might come to the gentiles through faith in Christ Jesus, so that by faith we might receive the promise of the Spirit."*

V19 "What then was the purpose of the Law? It was added because of transgressions until the seed to whom the promise referred had come."

The Law is not for the believer – grace is for the believer. Can you receive that into your spirit right now ? It is true. Don't be short-sighted because it will keep you from **seeing** the things that you are **hearing** about beyond your horizon.

DON'T RELY ON ILLUSIONS

Recently, I saw a programme that revealed the secrets of street magicians. It is not the first exposé that I have seen on magicians. When you see how they do their magic you cease to ask, 'How do they do that?' There is no wonder or amazement because every trick is simply an illusion – the simplicity of which often leaves one feeling amazed. It is difficult to believe that something that can hold the uninitiated spell-bound can be created so simply – what a con! The more experience I gain on this planet the more I think that nothing is as it seems, so much of what appears is really a con. Take people, how much of the real person is usually hidden behind the image of what we see and thus, perceive.

Another lesson that I learned recently was that of perspective. It was the story of a blind man who underwent an operation that resulted in him seeing only to tragically lose his sight again. However, the true story dealt with the fact that though the man could now physically see his brain held no perspective of what he was now seeing. This is really quite obvious but not something I had ever considered! Surely it is a different matter interpreting an object through its texture if you have previously seen it than it is if you have not previously seen it. But coordination between sight and texture cannot exist if a person has touched before he has seen. I was told in Africa that the average African has no concept of a good view or vista. But what is a good view? What is for you may not be for me?

Left to his own devices man will perceive reality whereas God reveals reality. Long before the relative normalisation of such things, as young sailors we would come across seemingly beautiful women who were really men. Don't be taken in by what you see, it may well be just an illusion. This is why many people think they have fallen in love when in reality they have gained an infatuation!

I wonder if this is why God ordained that faith should come by hearing and not by seeing. What we see is really open to interpretation, or levels of physical capabilities e.g. can a person with cataracts see the same shades as a fully sighted person? And at a spiritual level, what about seeing the faults of a person to the degree that you can no longer hear what God is saying through that person.

I wonder also if this is why people hear the Lord proportionately much more than people see Him. I mean is Jesus Black, Yellow, White or something in between?

Faith comes by hearing and hearing by the word of God. The word is jealously guarded by the Lord – detract or add to it at your peril – and surely it is so dependable because of its unchanging nature.

The eyes of the heart are meant to interpret what we see. When I lived in Tanzania I learned to buy things due to the person's worth rather than the worth of the goods. Maybe I had learned to see the vendors through the eyes of my heart. The apostle Paul said,

> *"I pray that the eyes of your heart maybe opened that you might know..."* Ephesians 1:18

Is this why the devil seeks to harden the hearts of unbelievers by causing us to harbour grievance or hold offence in our hearts. He is formidable at this – that is why Jesus had to command us to love at his level, 'Father, Do not hold this sin against them.' Don't allow what you are seeing to interpret either God or people for this is not God's way. Reality comes through the word which transcends human experience to the point that it delivers God's thoughts and ways into the heart of man.

Do you often have cause to exclaim, 'I've seen it all before!' truth is we all do because we all have to some degree.

As someone once rightly said, 'what we see is determined by what we are looking out from.' And as the heart is the wellspring of life we do well not to clog it up.

Raise your gaze above the haze and see that the sun is always shining above the clouds.

I guarantee if you allow God to open the eyes of your heart you will see both situations and people differently – including, importantly yourself. This is vital because when you see your position in Christ you will know that this will always overcome your condition in this world. If you take heed of what you hear from God you will begin to see all things differently – in fact you will begin to see in direct proportion to your readiness to hear and obey.

We may well sit side by side in the same church week after week but I have learned that we are definitely not all seeing the same things. As long as a person can hear from God he will eventually see.

What do people really see in you – I wonder if any of us are truly aware? Have you ever wondered what people repeatedly mention as you leave the scene? Grace and truth go hand in hand but truth is much more difficult to receive than grace is.

Oh the wonder that we are no longer under the law – it has served its intended purpose in your life by evangelising you because Jesus didn't come into the world to condemn it but rather that through him the world might be saved. You are under grace my friend realise it, rejoice in it and live accordingly. Heaven is prepared to receive you and it lasts forever, God will lay the red carpet out for you – yes you!

Put aside your own perspective because no doubt it has led to illusions and begin to see yourself from God's perspective. You are his child and when you fully realise this you will begin to treat others with the same level of love and grace that you have received. You are indeed standing under the canopy of amazing grace!

> Romans 6:15-23, *"What then? Shall we sin because we are not under law but under grace? By no means! Don't you know that when you offer yourselves to someone to obey him as slaves, you are slaves to the one whom you obey—whether you are slaves to sin, which leads to death, or to obedience, which leads to righteousness? But thanks be to God that, though you used to be slaves to sin, you wholeheartedly obeyed the form of teaching to which you were entrusted. You have been set free from sin and have become slaves to righteousness. I put this in human terms because you are weak in your natural selves. Just as you used to offer the parts of your body in slavery to impurity and to ever-increasing wickedness, so now offer them in slavery to righteousness leading to holiness. When you were slaves to sin, you were free from the control of righteousness. What benefit did you reap at that time from the things you are now ashamed of? Those things result in death! But now that you have been set free from sin and have become slaves to God, the benefit you*

reap leads to holiness, and the result is eternal life. For the wages of sin is death, but the gift of God is eternal life in Christ Jesus our Lord."

We are to live in God's grace by serving him unconditionally.

"The least in the kingdom of God is greater than John the Baptist." Matthew 11:11

Can we see that? Really see it. Once we see it then everything will change.

You see, to be least in the kingdom of God is to have infinitely more than the richest most successful person who is not in the kingdom of God. If we can for a moment understand heaven economically *(whether or not there will be money in heaven I don't know)* even if you only earn a pound a year in eternity it will accumulate to far more than even Bill Gates could earn in a lifetime on earth.

Think about it if you only save one pound a year in heaven – if you save it for a billion years you will become a billionaire and still have eternity to spend it.

'Now let the poor say I am rich'

Listen regularly to the language of faith because your mind is not neutral.

The deal is this - God asks us to submit to him now to the degree that he can live out his purpose through us. In simple terms, the gospel is as follows: we give him that now and he gives us all that then in addition to all the things that we need now.

You cannot live the Christian life, your only hope is to submit to the one who can and you submit to Christ by walking in the Spirit, thus, allowing him to live his life through you. Hear me, whoever you are, no matter what you have achieved at a human level, no matter how long you have been a Christian you cannot live the Christian life – you can merely submit to the one who can.

Once we realise that in order to be great in the kingdom we have to be prepared to be nobody in the world *(that is according to how the world sees it)*. Then we'll place ourselves at his feet. We will allow nothing to stop us from gaining his favour. A hard pill to swallow because we must take in faith that what God says is true is in fact true.

The kingdom of God is a kingdom of, grace, mercy, humility and love and these are some of the attributes that bring your personal greatness and success in the kingdom of God. The more you will humble yourself the greater you will become. The more truth you accept the more truth you will see. The more you are prepared to love the more power you will receive.

We must come by the Way of the Cross. The Cross means death before it means resurrection but every death in Christ is followed by a resurrection. The problem we face is our reluctance to accept death. You have died but unless you understand this you will never learn to walk in resurrection life.

We have an awful scene in the church today whereby, people are seeking to gain the anointing through earthly means, through talent and strong personality. We need talent and we need strength in personality but these are not the ingredients that gain the anointing. The anointing is gained through the condition of the heart. The heart begets true talent and the heart begets anointing.

Usually success in the world comes at the expense of the heart. So when the heart is tested we often fall back on the old nature and fail the test.

Oh how blinded we have been!

Folks - it is one thing being born again but it is entirely another thing to live life in the kingdom.

> *"For me to live is Christ – to die is gain."*
> Philippians 1:21

Don't speak the language of your emotions. And don't speak the language of defeat – neither belongs in the eternal kingdom of God. Doubt breeds doubt. Hear me again: the kingdom that you enter now is an eternal kingdom. Things are being worked out according to an eternal perspective.

You are, "More than a conqueror" when you feel like it and you are still more than a conqueror when you don't feel like it. You have conquered death because in Christ you have died already and been resurrected. Conviction still has a great role in your life but conviction is not condemnation – even though they might feel the same.

You are convicted when you are under grace and condemned when you are under law. As you are not under law your days of being condemned are over even though you are imperfect and are continuing to behave, at times, in a way that you are ashamed of. God is big enough to handle this – he is always good and Satan is always bad!

Jesus is the way, he is the truth, and therefore, he is the life.

Look beyond the sky and see a spiritual world that is beyond the ability of our senses to interpret. It is the parent world. It was here before the creation of matter. God is calling us to live back in the SUPERIOR and the Devil hates it! Break the chains and walk free. This is why when the word is sown as seed he wants to steal the seed before it has had chance to germinate and produce the immense potential that is contained in the seed.

We have a new day. You have a new day if you'll take it. Stop hearing God and dismissing it because of what you see. Wherever you live and whatever church you belong to, what you see will always get in the way of what you hear!

"Faith comes by hearing." By hearing and NOT BY SEEING! God knows that you will always interpret life by what you see. So he determined not to limit our expectations of him by what we see but rather we could go further by what we hear and believe. We have to move from hearing to listening and from listening to doing, and then we can move on to the next level. If you hear and obey God will open the eyes of your heart so that you can see!

So if God says, *"He took up my sickness and my infirmity."* It is not enough to disprove this just because you haven't seen it. Faith will not submit to scientific analysis or the traditions and expectancy of man because faith is superior to scientific analysis.

True preaching is not telling about God it is saying what God is saying.

We don't believe because the previous generation didn't believe and they didn't believe because the generation before them didn't believe... Somebody has got to start believing. Preaching fell under the spell of this world and became a matter of pride and eloquence rather than the, 'telling forth from God.'

How fickle we can be, we say, 'preach it brother' until what is being preached affects us! Then there is a strange silence. That's why any preacher worth his weight will take platitudes from man with a pinch of salt.

The Bible was inspired by the Holy Spirit and written by scribes thousands of years ago but it is still living today.

There are no sight barriers between you and a visiting speaker, you have visibly seen the mistakes and weaknesses of your pastor but usually not those of a visiting preacher, therefore, you readily hear what he is saying even though often he is only saying what you have been hearing from your pastor.

Faith comes by hearing because some of us can't see beyond today.

Don't miss out on what he is saying because of what you are seeing!

If you can see it, it's not permanent.

> *"But my righteous one will live by faith and if he shrinks back I will not pleased by him."* Heb. 10:38

"For in the gospel a righteousness from God is revealed, a righteousness that is by faith from first to last, just as it is written: The righteous will live by faith." Rom.1:17

Do we believe we are just? "Just" simply means 'right standing in Christ'

Those who know they are **just** no longer have to **justify** themselves.

The just believe what God says about them not what people think.

We have so much but there are barriers to what we are receiving.

Faith must go beyond what we see.

We come through and **into.**

You will only live in the power of the new to the degree that you will let go of the old. Come on now!!! Come to the cross and reckon. Realise these following words:

"If any man be in Christ Jesus he is a new creation, the old has gone, behold all things are new." 2 Corinthians 5:17

You have to believe that what took place at Calvary as it pertains to you when you come to the cross actually took place. The Apostle Paul was not the only one who has been crucified with Christ. You have been crucified with Christ and so have I. The difference is in realisation ... Once you realise it you have begun the process of living accordingly. The old has gone so don't resurrect it! Walk away from your past and into the provision of your future in God. You have a choice live in the old even though it has been crucified or actively put off the old and live in the new.

Your strength in God will be in direct proportion to the condition of your heart.
Sin has been dealt with vicariously. It was God who initiated it and completed it himself without our help or even our concession. Self is a different matter.

The fact that your sins have been dealt with has given you access into the kingdom of God - the parallel kingdom. Access into it does not guarantee that you will live successfully in it. Self is now your problem.

The missionary Jim Elliot said,

'live in such away that when it's time to die all that you have to do is to die.'

Adopt the following attitude towards all people, 'I disagree with what you do but not with you.' Recognise the times when God comes to test you and don't side with Satan by allowing your Christian walk to lose its passion. The stretching comes only so that you can contain more of God.

Man was created in the image of God. This was tarnished by the fall. But salvation means that you can regain this – ALL OF IT.

> Eph.4:22-24, *"You were taught, with regard to your former way of life, to put off your old self, which is being corrupted by its deceitful desires; to be made new in the attitude of your minds; and to put on the new self, created to be like God in true righteousness and holiness".*

Put off the old instead of allowing it to live side by side with the new. It cannot co-exist. There is a bridge from the old over to the new and that bridge is to be found in:

> v23, **"To be made new in the attitude of your minds"**

So don't feed your old self – there are some things that the new self will refuse to be fed on. Therefore, the old has no place in feeding the new it will only succeed in nourishing and adding strength to the pull of the old man. In order for the new self to grow and mature we must find out what nourishes it.

Originally, man was made in the image of God. At the fall the image was lost. But when we are saved the new self is created to be like God in true righteousness and holiness. Righteousness has been credited to you but holiness has not. Holiness happens as we are restored into the image of God. This means we become like him in character. This is not beyond us – it is what God expects from all of us because that is where the true benefits of our adoption are realised.

Get the beginning point and in the future you will find that what you have prayed then is happening now. What you confessed then is happening now.

One **and** one make two. You can't fully understand this until you have walked through the **and**….

There are reasons why God answers prayers and responds to confessions of faith and there are reasons why he does not. Do what is necessary to find out why God answers prayer. It is not worth holding on to the past - deal with it ruthlessly.

This mean we will have to change our lifestyles in order to put off so that we can 'cross the bridge, to be made new in the attitude of your minds; before we can put on the new self created to be like God.

We cannot see what is yonder beyond the bridge but we can hear about and pursue it. In fact the bridge does not really exist. It is a figment in the mind of the natural man. God does not use bridges he uses more spiritual means. Hear and follow! When I was looking to God to answer the intricate questions surrounding my situation all I could hear was: *trust, follow and obey.* It was enough.

At any given time the following is true - we have not yet become all that we are. This is true of you and it is true of me.

There is a practical solution. Having realised our present condition we must obey the following injunction:

> *"Do not offer the parts of your body to sin, as instruments of wickedness, but rather offer yourselves to God, as those who have been brought from death to life; and offer the parts of your body to him as instruments of righteousness. For sin shall not be your master, because you are not under law, but under grace."* Romans 6:13-14

Sin is not a good paymaster but you must fill your life with righteousness or you will slide into its web – guaranteed! Let me repeat something vital here. If you are a Christian you must realise that you are no longer under Law but under grace. The reason for this is clear – law has served its purpose in evangelizing you i.e. making you conscious of your need of a Saviour! Allow the grace you now stand in to launch you into realising your potential.

It is time to put SELF on the line and sign the consent form so that God can help you to put off in order to put on.

If you are still anchored in the old self you will have to put up with the dominion that the old self lived in but there is something infinitely better. Realise that self must die so that you can begin to live the eternal now!

Chapter 7

DELIVER US FROM EVIL

Everything that we will ever need was obtained for us at Calvary. The potential for you to find healing and deliverance is already in place it is a case of finding it in God.

Do you walk daily in the realisation that you, being in Christ, have authority over all the power of the evil one? Read on and understand...

> Here is a clue: *"No good thing does he withhold from those whose walk is blameless."* Psalm 84:11

We have an enemy who does not want us to receive all that is rightfully ours "In Christ".

This book is really about foundations and the reason for it is this - in order to receive the abundant life that God has promised we must not be deceived about the necessary foundations. The ingredient by which we now live as children of God is faith and as we have just seen faith does not come by seeing it comes by hearing and hearing by the word of God. So our future is dependant on what we hear *(from God)* and not by what we see around us.

What we see then has to be passed through our hearts. So the Apostle Paul prayed,

"I pray that God would open the eyes of your hearts so that you might see"

In the kingdom, hearing only becomes seeing when we pass what we hear from God through the eyes of hearts that are loving God and man at God's intended level. This is the fourth dimension that is available to believers.

We are to look at the world around us and the people around us through the eyes of our hearts. What we are looking out from determines what we see. In addition God has given us an unpolluted language to use. Reinhardt Bonnke says, 'Speaking in tongues means that spiritual truths take on physical character.'

We have an enemy and we need to understand his tactics.

Rather than being a mere personification of evil, there can be no doubt that Satan is revealed to us in Scripture as a created, intelligent being.

So when the Lord's Prayer teaches us to pray:

"Deliver us from the evil one." Matthew 6:13

We are asking the Lord to free us from the effects of an intelligent adversary who is set against us.

The meaning of his names gives us tremendous insight into his nature.

1. "Satan" means adversary or opposer.
2. "Devil" means slanderer.
3. "The Evil one" denotes the essence of his character.
4. "The Serpent" indicates his guile and craftiness.

One of Satan's activities is to be the accuser of the brethren. He does this unceasingly and he has a good case against us because we do sin. However, the death of Jesus covered all sin – big and small - because sin is a condition and Jesus death cleansed us from the affect of the **condition**. Therefore, we are defended on the sole basis that **all** our sins were paid for by Christ's death when he paid for SIN!

During my dark night of the soul I understood the above in theory but I had not made it my own. I was hearing the voice of Satan but he was imitating the voice of the Lord. This voice would constantly tell me the worst – it would convince me of horrendous things that were coming my way and that I deserved them. Finally, the voice swore at me and I knew at once that the Lord would not swear. You must realise that I was sleepless and my mind was foggy and depressed.

Satan is also the tempter. He tempted Eve, he tempted Jesus and he tempts all believers particularly into immorality. (*See 1 Cor. 7:5*)

Satan is described as, *"The ruler of this world."* (*John 12:31*)

He is, *"The god of this world."* (*2 Cor. 4:4*)

He is, *"The prince of the power of the air."* (*Eph.2:2*)

1 John 5:19, *"The whole world is under is control."*

Rev. 12:9, *"He deceives the whole world."*

Eph. 6:12, *"He resides in the air (the heavenly places)."*

He is ruler of the COSMOS for this AGE.

Ryrie said, 'The cosmos is that organized framework of things in which mankind lives and moves and which opposes God by eliminating him and counterfeiting him.'

That kind of rule is fearsome apart from the fact that:

> *"Greater is he that is in us than he that is in the world."* 1 John 4:4

In Summary:

Satan:
Background: Accuser, adversary, tempter.

Looks: Serpent, dragon.

Characteristics: Liar, murderer, ruler.

Activities: accuses tempts, destroys.

This powerful, intelligent being must not be underestimated.

The nature of Satan's sin is reflected to us in 1 Tim. 3:6

His sin was arrogance, conceit, being puffed up. Not far removed from the sin a new believer might have when he is pushed forward or asserts himself too quickly and begins to take the glory that is God's alone. This is why the commands to love cover all types of sin. The way to unlock the promises of God is to find the keys of humility, grace, mercy, love - in short to walk in the fruit of the spirit.

> *"Submit yourselves then to God. Resist the Devil and he will flee from you."* James 4:7

If you perceive that you are under attack then the first thing to do is not to attack Satan but to submit to God.

Learn to enquire of God, 'what is Satan doing concerning me?' Your heavenly Father will not withhold such information from you.

SATAN'S ACTIVITIES

The various names attributed to Satan ought to tell us that he can attack us in various ways, using diverse tactics. The essence of Satan's activity against God is to offer a rival kingdom and programme. This battle is being fought in the mind of mankind in every nation on our planet.

Three general areas that you might be under attack:

- Conform to the pressures and structure of society.
- You may be tempted to cover up selfish actions.
- You may be tempted into immorality.

THE ADVERSARY

Remember that sin and law walk hand in hand and lead us towards a wrong perception of judgement. As we have seen, Satan is, *"the accuser of the brethren."* His aim is to nullify our witness of the gospel by quenching our understanding of eternal grace. This is why it is imperative that we are *rooted and grounded in love.*

Firstly, he seeks to turn governmental authority against us. He will imprison or even kill believers. He creates an atmosphere of fear, to the point that we will hide what we are.

Secondly, Satan spotlights our sins. Notice I said **sins** and not sin. I re-emphasise this so that you will realise that your sins were massed into the condition of sin and that is what Jesus died for. He died for sin so that you could be saved from your sins. Your sins *(plural)* were incorporated into the sin *(singular)* at the cross when Christ became sin.

How I needed to know that because our enemy will get us to concentrate on the sins that you have personally committed even convincing you that some were so bad that God couldn't possibly forgive you... Jesus didn't simply die for your sins, he died for sin! He covered every sin ever committed by every person such was the atonement carried out by Jesus. Allow that truth to help you – it is mind blowing and will convince you that you have not committed the unpardonable sin.

> *"If you confess your sin to the Lord (any sin)*
> *he is faithful and just to forgive you of your*
> *sin and to cleanse you from all*
> *unrighteousness."* 1 John 1:9

I need to add in response to the above as I write this, a very personal, 'Praise the lord!'

Our understanding of this is one of the greatest battles we need to win.

I say again to you child of God: you need to listen to the language of faith and learn to speak it. This will have a devastating affect on your life. God has brought you out of the kingdom of darkness and into his wonderful light. He did not and has not made a mistake. Are you experiencing the benefits of the light or are you still ensnared by the deceit of the darkness. Why be a pauper when you are a joint heir with Christ. That is not a rhetorical question, take time to ponder it and seek to answer it. Why?

Chapter 8

THE COSMOS

The cosmos *(world)* has several meanings but generally in the New Testament it is used to describe, 'this world, as it is set apart from God and functioning according to its own light and reason.'

It is: the ordered whole that is separate from God.

Ryrie says of the cosmos:

'The cosmos *(world)* is that system organised by Satan, and run by Satan, which leaves God out and is rival to him.'

There is a counterfeit order on our planet headed up by Satan. If we could see the degree that we are all pawns in this system and the way it is linked to world politics we would all gladly and hurriedly submit ourselves to the kingdom of God. The inherent evil of the cosmos is not that it is out and out darkness *(it contains good things as well as bad)* but rather that it is completely independent of the creator God!

In James 4:4 we are told that friendship with the world *(cosmos)* is hostility toward God.

1 John 2:16, *"All that is in the world is not from the Father"*.

The main pull and attractiveness of the cosmos is that it seeks to place self as number one and the here and now as the most important.

> *"Do not love the world or anything in the world, if anyone loves the world, the love of the Father is not in him. For everything in the world, the cravings of sinful man, the lust of his eyes and the boasting of what he has and does comes not from the Father but from the cosmos (world)."* 1 John 2:15-16

Satan is at work in tempting us to seek satisfaction as our top priority.

He urges us to satisfy the lusts of the flesh try and get what your eyes make you first desire and then covet and build a self-sufficient pride and arrogance by boasting about your possessions. This is the prevailing philosophy of our world and it has no place in the church *(the kingdom of God)*. So we have understood that Satan seeks to divert our thinking by getting us to place self first and the here and now *(the temporary)* as the most important. Whereby, the gospel teaches that God is first and that eternity is most important. God knows that our thinking needs to change to the degree that our automatic response becomes a Godly one.

"The word of the Lord stands forever."

God has already passed sentence on the cosmos it will be judged and terminated. In fact it will take only one day to destroy it.

The kingdom of God offers us a different foundation to live by – The Royal Law. The Royal Law is meant to gird us up and to open a door into the supernatural thus, providing all that we need in a world that is diametrically opposed to the children of God - a world that gravitates in the opposite direction.

One dramatic failing in the body of Christ is that we have not seen the absolute imperative of having the Royal Law in place before we seek to operate the "Gifts of the Spirit". So what we have seen in the main is an insipid and ineffective usage of the gifts that can often be governed by 1 John 2:16 rather than the fruit of the Spirit.

Life in the kingdom has unparalleled benefits but only if you live by the principles of the kingdom. God asks us to make our choices!

The fruit and gifts that are available in the kingdom are sufficient for the total care of its inhabitants. Christ likeness in this cosmos means separation from this cosmos. Separation is not isolation but it is separation. Our service and attitude toward God and life must not live alongside our old values but rather **replace** them. The full benefits of the kingdom will only be realised as we learn to do this.

God wants us to act in such a way that it will cause others to have testimony that will bring attention and ultimate glory to him. Become an untouchable by living within the confines of the kingdom. This is not a geographical statement but rather a behavioural one. We must behave in such a way that we live beyond the reaches of the tentacles of the evil one! Don't make a truce with the Devil – he is not honourable the only thing he understands is the implementation of Christ's total victory. Don't give him a day off concerning your life; live in such away that you can hound him continuously.

Living in the kingdom of God is a matter of choice.

It is no use living in this cosmos to the degree that we cannot take authority over its ruler. When you move into another kingdom you have to adapt to its differences – you can no longer live with some of the principles and traditions of the old kingdom. People are held by illusions. These illusions are created by this world – the cosmos and they create perceptions of reality, whereby, the Scriptures give us a revelation of reality.

The Royal Law is the foundation of the kingdom.

"So, in everything do unto others what you would have them do to you, for this sums up the Law and the Prophets." Matt. 7:12

The Baptism in the Holy Spirit is the empowering of the kingdom.

"You will receive power when the Holy Spirit comes on you." Acts 1:8

The Gifts of the Holy Spirit are the ongoing supernatural provision of the kingdom.

"So I say live by the Spirit and you will not gratify the desires of the sinful nature." Galatians 5:16

We have been crucified with Christ and baptised into his resurrection. We have then been empowered by the Baptism in the Holy Spirit which is the doorway to being filled with the power of God.

Go on being filled so that we can operate in both the natural and supernatural giftings of the kingdom.

1 Cor. 12:7-11, *"Now to each one the manifestation of the Spirit is given for the common good. To one there is given through the Spirit the message of wisdom, to another the message of knowledge by*

means of the same Spirit, to another faith by the same Spirit, to another gifts of healing by that one Spirit, to another miraculous powers, to another prophecy, to another distinguishing between spirits, to another speaking in different kinds of tongues, and to still another the interpretation of tongues. All of these are the work of one and the same Spirit, and he gives them to each one, just as he determines."

Rom 12:5-8, *"So in Christ we who are many form one body, and each member belongs to all the others. We have different gifts, according to the grace given us. If a man's gift is prophesying let him use it in proportion to his faith. If it is serving, let him serve; if it is teaching, let him teach; if it is encouraging, let him encourage; if it is contributing to the needs of others, let him give generously; if it is leadership, let him govern diligently; if it is showing mercy, let him do it cheerfully."*

Some of these gifts are evident in today's church but where are the rest? God's children are supposed to have supernatural provision but there are obstacles in the way. The evil one wants to stop the flow of God's love, anointing and power flowing through the body and transforming individual lives. So we must get the Royal Law in place and then stop making a **truce** with sinful habits.

What is a truce? It is making a treaty by allowing the god of this world to still govern part of your behaviour. It is time to claim victory in the areas where you have made a truce! Hope will keep us moving in the right direction.

"If you can't fly, run. If you can't run, walk. If you can't walk, crawl, but by all means keep moving." Martin Luther King Jr. used to tell his civil rights workers.

Jim Elliot the missionary martyr once observed that many Christians are so intent on doing something for God that they forget God's main work is to make something of them.

All that you observe around you has no permanence so learn to think differently about it. Forever is forever and you will be alive forevermore. Allow this to govern your choices.

It's as simple as this - each day set your goals to love God by loving people. Give yourself a reminder that this is truly what God is looking for and that he will cause every good thing to come your way if only you will keep his commands to love.

Chapter 9

CITIZENS OF HEAVEN

"But our citizenship is in heaven and we eagerly await a saviour from there, the Lord Jesus Christ." Philippians 3:20

The word "citizenship" is very important here because it signifies something special. It signifies a colony of foreigners who though living in a foreign country live by the laws of their own country and model their lives after their native home.

Philippi was of course a Roman colony whose inhabitants though not actually in Rome lived as though they were. They dressed like Romans, talked like Romans and even thought like Romans. If we go to most parts of the world we will see the British doing the same. At the moment I am writing this in Arusha, Tanzania our former home that we are visiting at the moment. One of the beauties of Tanzania is that it is still possible to observe a culture that has not been tarnished by the modern world. There are many people living today as their ancestors lived thousands of years ago. Still, even here, the ex-pat community show signs of their European way of life. In other words we maintain the culture of another place in the face of the abiding culture and ways.

So Paul's statement *"citizens of heaven"* meant we are to live according to the laws of heaven rather than the laws of earth.

Heaven and its blessings are **now** in terms of our spiritual experience. The oxygen of the kingdom is love.

By this will all men know that we are his disciples, that we have love one for another.

Is this how the world recognises us? If not why not? Have we missed something?

LIFE IN THE HEAVENLIES

Eph.1:3, *"Praise be to the God and Father of our Lord Jesus Christ, who has blessed us with every spiritual blessing in the heavenly realms, in Christ Jesus."*

The location is "The Heavenlies". That is where Christ is seated.

"Which he exerted in Christ when he raised him from the dead and seated him at his right hand in the heavenly realms." Eph.1:20

This is also where the believer is seated.

"And God raised us up with Christ and seated us with him in the heavenly realms in Christ Jesus." Eph. 2:6

It is also the place of blessings.

"Who has blessed us with every spiritual blessing in the heavenly realms, in Christ Jesus." Eph.1:3

"EVERY"

We are to learn how to bring heaven's blessing into the earth's atmosphere

"For our struggle is not against flesh and blood but against the authorities against the powers of this dark world and against the spiritual forces of darkness of evil in the heavenly realms." Eph. 6:10

It is God saying this so it is not presumption.

Now if these were the blessings of God in the "earthlies" as opposed to the "heavenlies" then they could be obtained by earthly means.

Earthly means to gain heavens blessing.

But as they are located in the "heavenlies" they can be acquired by heavenly means only. If we are to bring the blessings of God to earth, we must live by the laws of heaven. If you keep the laws of heaven you will keep the laws of the land. God has deposited the riches of heaven in our account, but unless we know how to write cheques on that account we will spend our days in spiritual poverty.

So the big question is: how? How do we move the blessings of heaven into our earth now? How do we make what is ours positionally ours experientially? How, having been rooted and established in love *(at God's required level)* can we draw on the vast wealth that is now available to us direct from heaven?

> The answer to all of these "hows" is the same it's **faith!**
>
> *"The only thing that counts is faith expressing itself through love."* Galatians 6:9

Faith is the substance from heaven – love is the law of heaven.

Everything that Christ has done for the believer is ABSOLUTE but it must be APPROPRIATED.

Absolute means, 'perfectly independent of anything else to sustain it, self- existent and unlimited.'

Appropriate means, 'to take as one's own – to take possession'.

All of God's promises are absolute: *"Yes and Amen"*

So the sacrificial death of Christ is absolute in that nothing else is required for man's salvation and that his death is for every man. God's love in Christ was directed to the whole world.

> *"For God so loved the world."* John 3:16

> John 1:29, *"Behold the lamb of God who takes away the sin of the whole world."*

> 1 John 2:2, *"He is the atoning sacrifice for our sins, and not only for ours, but also for the sins of the whole world."*

This absolute atonement has to be appropriated by faith.

In simple terms: believing activates the promise…

"He who does not believe is condemned already." John 3:18

If we can understand this principle then we can understand the principle of faith. We receive because we believe. When Jesus came to earth he began to preach, *"The kingdom of God is at hand."*

His message was: the age to come has come and he demonstrated it by his power over, disease, the devil and death. These two ages run side by side – the age to come began almost 2000 years ago in Bethlehem that's why Colossians 1:13 says, we have already been delivered from the dominion of darkness: *"For he has rescued us from the dominion of darkness and into the kingdom of the Son he loves."*

We have tasted some of the powers of the coming age but not yet all of the powers of the coming age – maybe it is time that we did.

Jesus himself taught us to pray:

"Your will be done on earth as it is in heaven."

Obviously heaven can touch earth now or this prayer is a mockery.

However, heavens blessings will only come to earth now to the degree that we live by heavens laws now.

Bible teacher J. Oswald Sanders said, 'The function of faith is to turn God's promises into fact.'

Live the Royal Law, pray for the promise, believe that you will receive it and you will.

Here is the Scriptural evidence:
> *"Therefore, I tell you, whatever you ask for in prayer, believe that you have received it and it will be yours. And when you stand praying, if you hold anything against anyone, forgive him so that your heavenly father may forgive your sins."* Mark 11:24-25

More about this later!

We can see that the Royal Law **links** heaven to earth and earth back to heaven. Living by heaven's law opens the door for the promise of God to be realised on earth. Confidence is built when we live as citizens of heaven now during our sojourn on earth.

Once we are receiving the promises of God it ought to be obvious to all who are in contact with our lives. You and I are God's best evangelistic programme. Do people want what they see that you have?

How much time and effort should we be putting in to the cultivation of the Royal Law?

Chapter 10

LOVE LETTERS

You have a king – Jesus – he represents authority and power..

You have a counsellor – Jesus - he represents wisdom and understanding.

The living God is there for us always – *"an ever present help in times of need."* Sometimes we will need to rely on his power and authority – sometimes we will need to rely on his wisdom to gain perspective. Do people see the reality of your faith? Do they see that you are stable and walk in authority, power, wisdom and understanding?

God intended that you should be a letter. When people read you they should at all times read what you are capable of. You are capable of love, don't aim for things that you are not capable of in yourself, aim for the things that you are and the rest will surely follow.

2 Corinthians 3:2-3, *"You yourselves are our letter, written on our hearts, known and read by everybody. You show that you are a letter from Christ, the result of our ministry, written not with ink but with the Spirit of the living God, not on tablets of stone but on tablets of human hearts."*

You must be prepared to be read by God quietly but, at times, by people out loud. This is discipleship! So often dark experiences are the way in which God will bring us to a place whereby we can accept his counsel coming to us through a human agent. Why do we allow so much pride to exist in our midst? It is surely a killer of life.

Because we have allowed people to choose whether to be a disciple or not we now have the scenario where those who want to be disciples carry a tremendous weight in those who belong but do not want to be disciples. I repeat if you are a follower of Christ you have an obligation to God and his body on earth. You are being read so what is being read? Perhaps we do not realise the significance of this. Once you become a Christian you will either gather or scatter people.

"We can be filled to all the fullness of Christ" so that, *"we will be mature and complete, not lacking anything."* Nobody but you can stop this happening.

So is that what is being read in you?

We should not be satisfied until this is what people read in us. Light up your neighbourhood by fulfilling your obligation to God. To love at his level is both the minimum and maximum requirement.

This is another reason why we face trials, God knows human nature only too well – we will not grow until we are stretched. We must continue to be stretched so that we can contain more of God. And this means we must place ourselves in a position where we will be stretched. The person who has been severely stretched will accept God on his terms – nothing else is important, I know because I have been there.

Two things are important here:

1)   We must learn to walk a straight line despite the trials and circumstances that beset us.
2)   The reason for this is that we are *"Living letters"* read by all.

God wants us to be an alternative society which is achieved by adopting the ways of the kingdom of God thus, leading us to be counter-culture and not simply a sub-culture.

Under the **Old Covenant** God raised up one nation Israel and gave them his law. They were the only nation on earth who had the Law of God. God told them that if they **kept the Law** they would be a chosen nation amongst nations and all other nations would see that they were a **counter-culture.** Thereby, recognising God through this one nation

Only the keeping of the entire law, as given through Moses and recorded in Deuteronomy, would give them the **nature** that God required. They had to keep every single part of the law. They would be like a living letter, read by the nations. Of course, as intended by God, they failed to do this *(he knew that it was impossible)*, thus, entered the **New Covenant** through the shedding of the blood of God's Son, Jesus Christ. Now the church was to be the **counter-culture** but instead of keeping the Mosaic Law the New Covenant people were simply to keep the **Royal Law**. The very nature of Christ would be imparted into the believer so that all believers could live out the Royal Law through a process of believing and making choices to walk in the spirit.

> Aren't you glad that our God doesn't say, 'If you hate and try to wipe out the heathen the world will know that you belong to me.'

> *"Do not judge and you will not be judged, do not condemn and you will not be condemned. Forgive and you will be forgiven. Give and it will be given to you. A good measure pressed down, shaken together and running over, will be poured into your lap. For with the measure you use it will be measured to you."* Luke 6:37

John 3:14 *"We know that we have passed from death to life because we love our brothers. Anyone who does not love remains in death."*

Unconditional love is the greatest power in the universe - it causes earthquakes, people to come out of their graves and inanimate objects to tear. Yet, we are usually so poor at living out this side of Christian life that we have no proof of life in this direction. It is high time that we did have proof of life at this level. Why not? Are we expecting God to move in power when we will not forgive people for far less than God has had to forgive us for?

We owe a debt of love at this level.

On the eve of my going into hospital which subsequently led to my darkest days I had a dream whereby Debbie and I were facing creatures that we had never seen before. We could not escape them and didn't know what to do about them. This seemed to go on for an age and gradually became worse until I was experiencing a nightmare. It seemed like nothing I could do could help me until suddenly the presence of God came on the scene and brought peace into the midst of the chaos. The following morning the words 'When the presence comes the problems will disappear.' were implanted in my spirit.

This is how we receive from God even if the receipt of such things brings no immediate relief or victory. The seed of victory has now been sown into the spirit.

Around that time I also had a vision in which I was sitting in a stately home with God. I was in a very big room that resembled a library. In the background was a wall library that contained all the knowledge that mankind had gleaned since the creation. This wall of books seemed never ending and was hugely impressive that is until I looked at God who was sitting between me and the books. As I looked from this angle the books became miniscule in light of his presence. Secondly, on the table was a globe atlas of the world. It impressed me as the biggest globe atlas that I had ever seen, then God picked it up and it became miniscule in the palm of his hand. The final thing I saw was a jigsaw laid flatly on the table the jigsaw was of human DNA. God quickly finished the puzzle and it lay complete on the table. But it was only as God breathed on it that it became three dimensional and took upon itself life.

God was speaking to me about seeing him in a dimension that I had never seen him before. In order to come out of my darkness I would have to find him in this dimension. The fact however remains when revelation lands in the spirit of a person it may not initially bring about change. This is because it has landed in seed form and it is only as the seed is watered and begins to germinate that the results appear. This truth became implanted in my heart over a period of time. What a vital, life giving lesson.

Chapter 11

THE LAW IS MADE OBSOLETE

The Law cannot and was never meant to save us. I have already mentioned this but lets look at it more fully.

Hebrews 7:11—*"If perfection could have been attained through the Levitical priesthood (for on the basis of it the law was given to the people), why was there still need for another priest to come—one in the order of Melchizedek, not in the order of Aaron? For when there is a change of the priesthood, there must also be a change of the law. He of whom these things are said belonged to a different tribe, and no one from that tribe has ever served at the altar. For it is clear that our Lord descended from Judah, and in regard to that tribe Moses said nothing about priests. And what we have said is even more clear if another priest like Melchizedek appears, one who has become a priest not on the basis of a regulation as to his ancestry but on the basis of the power of an indestructible life. For it is declared: "You are a priest forever, in the order of Melchizedek. The former regulation is set aside because it was weak and useless (for the law made nothing perfect), and a better hope is introduced, by which we draw near to God. And it was not without an oath! Others became priests without any oath, but he became a priest with an oath when God said to him: The Lord has sworn and will not change his mind: You are a priest forever.' "*

Because of this oath, Jesus has become the guarantee of a better covenant.

Now there have been many of those priests, since death prevented them from continuing in office; but because Jesus lives forever, he has a permanent priesthood. Therefore he is able to save completely those who come to God through him, because he always lives to intercede for them.

Such a high priest meets our need—one who is holy, blameless, pure, set apart from sinners, exalted above the heavens. Unlike the other high priests, he does not need to offer sacrifices day after day, first for his own sins, and then for the sins of the people. He sacrificed for their sins once for all when he offered himself. For the law appoints as high priests men who are weak; but the oath, which came after the law, appointed the Son, who has been made perfect forever."

The law of God cannot save and what is more it was never meant to save. It is in fact impossible to please God by trying to keep the Law of God.

THE THREE PRIESTHOODS

The first is the mysterious figure Melchizadek whose name means King of Righteousness; High Priest over the Gentiles.

We first meet Melchizadek in Genesis. 14:18, *"Then Melchizadek king of Salem brought out bread and wine. He was Priest of God most high."*

Then again in Psalm 110:4

This Priesthood was from the beginning – before there were any Jews on earth. Therefore, it was priesthood for the non Jew.

The second was the Levitical Priesthood in the line of Aaron this was the Priesthood over the Jews. This Priesthood was formed as the Jews became a nation and was for the Jews alone.

The third, Jesus Christ who is the **Great** High Priest over Jew and Gentile and came in the order of Melchizadek.

"The Law of the Spirit of life in Christ Jesus has set me free from the Law of Sin and Death. For what the Law was powerless to do in that it was weakened by the sinful nature God did by sending his own Son in the likeness of sinful man to be a sin offering." Romans 8:1-3

The Law is a religious thing but it is not a Christian thing. Through man's lack of understanding we have embraced the Law into Christendom when there is something far superior for us.

John the Baptist was the last in the line of the Levitical Priests. His Father Zechariahs was a Priest. The Priesthood had become corrupted as the Romans, the occupying forces, had appointed the present High priest. Therefore, John the Baptist was the one who baptised Jesus.

You are a Royal Priesthood a Holy Nation a people belonging to God.

"He who is least in the kingdom of God is greater than John the Baptist."
If growth came by the keeping of the law the methods God would use to enable us to grow would simply be the keeping of the Law. However, because this was never his intention he has a far better method to enable us to grow.

True growth comes during those times when God has distanced himself from us. When we have to search for him and take measures that we have never had to take before. For example, when God stands on the water and says, *"get out of the boat and come."* Just as long as Peter had his mind set on what he was heading to he managed to walk on water but as soon as his mind wandered to what he was going through he began to sink.

The elite Special Air Services of the British Army do much of their training on the Brecon Beacons near where we live. One part of their training is long, excruciating marches through rough terrain and carrying kit. The SAS pride themselves on both their physical and their mental fitness and they are amongst the crack troops in the world. It is known that as the soldiers think they have finished their marches and arrive at the recovery trucks in a state of exhaustion the trucks will drive off forcing the soldiers to go further than they imagined they would and, more important, than they thought they could.

Real growth comes when we allow God to stretch our faith – so he sets up the process by using trials, challenges and circumstances. All off a basis of unconditional love.

You can yet go much further than you thought you would or could.

Catch the following and you will go and do much more than you thought was possible.

> The Bible says, *"Your faith which is of greater worth than gold."* 1 Peter 1:7

> Romans10:4 informs us, *"Christ is the end of the Law so that there may be righteousness for everyone who believes."* Who believes!

Jesus Christ came in the order of Melchizadek not the order of Aaron.

> Rom. 3:21, *"But now a righteousness from God, apart from Law, has been made known, to which the Law and the prophets testify. This righteousness from God comes through faith in Jesus Christ to all who believe there is no difference."*

So what then was God's purpose in giving the Levitical Law through Moses?

> This is answered for us in Romans. 3:19, which says, *"Now we know that whatever the Law says, it says to those who are under the Law so that every mouth may be*

silenced and the whole world held accountable to God. Therefore, no-one will be declared righteous in his sight by observing the Law; rather through the Law we become conscious of sin."

There can be no conversion without conviction.

"For all have sinned and fall short of the glory of God." Romans 3:23

There's the damning conviction.

Here comes the amazing grace; *"And are justified freely by his grace through the redemption that came by Christ Jesus."*

This Christ is now able to save completely those who come to him. Come to him – whether they are Jew, Hindu, Muslim or nothing.

Listen again: *"Now there have been many of those priests, since death prevented them from continuing in office; but because Jesus lives forever, he has a permanent priesthood. Therefore he is able to save completely those who come to God through him, because he always lives to intercede for them.*
Such a high priest meets our need—one who is holy, blameless, pure, set apart from

sinners, exalted above the heavens. Unlike the other high priests, he does not need to offer sacrifices day after day, first for his own sins, and then for the sins of the people. He sacrificed for their sins once for all when he offered himself. For the law appoints as high priests men who are weak; but the oath, which came after the law, appointed the Son, who has been made perfect forever."

Folks you are not under Law you are under grace and you also have a Great high priest who is interceding for you. You are heaven bound forever. If he has done all this on earth for you imagine what it will be like in heaven.

You are heading for heaven but eternal life begins now. You can enjoy it to the fullest degree. We are going to see the extravagant expectations of those who are seeking to keep the Royal Law which is the doorway into the Promised Land.

Chapter 12

MAN CANNOT LIVE BY BREAD ALONE

God will put immense pressure on us so that we will go further than we have ever been.

"Man does not live on bread alone but by every word that proceeds from the mouth of God."

Notice something here – does not. However well we are living we are not living to our maximum potential unless we are living by every word that proceeds from the mouth of God.

The Bible tells us:
"The word of God is living and active..."
Hebrews 4:12

And in John 6:63 *"The Spirit gives life the flesh counts for nothing the words that I have spoken are Spirit and they are life!"*

If bread or food provides us with life and health - then can God's word have the same affect? I think so!

Listen to Proverbs 4:20, which says, *"My son pay attention to my words, do not let them out of your sight, for they are life to those who find them and health to a man's whole body."*

That is quite a claim isn't it? The Word of God equates to life and health.
Is there more to this than we have understood?

If we are keeping the Royal Law then can we expect to receive life, health and **whatsoever** from the word of God?

Scientific healing comes from outside of us in the form of medication etc. But has God devised a way by which we can receive healing through His Word and His Spirit on the inside?

"Seek first the kingdom of God and his righteousness and all these things will be added unto you." Matthew 6:33

How do we do this? Well we do it by getting hold of the keys of the kingdom.

Take the keys and unlock the doorway into the riches and resources of the kingdom. Note this says, "keys **of** the kingdom" not keys **to** the kingdom.

Having gained entrance to the kingdom through Jesus Christ there has to be a taking a pressing in, a getting hold **of** the keys of the kingdom!

We need to know what gives us access to the riches of the kingdom! Having gained access to the kingdom, living in it is what matters.

Dallas Willard says, 'We need a key of the keys.' So what is that key of the keys?

The Apostle Paul prayed, *"I pray that the eyes of your heart would be enlightened (opened) that you may know..."*

The natural eye sees circumstance and forms its pictures of reality. The eyes of your heart see perspective and allow it to determine reality: vision, aspect and status.

The abundance of God is not passively received, and does not happen by chance. The abundance of God is claimed and put into action by our active, intelligent pursuit of it.

May we enter a period of enjoyment of **access.** He won't manifest his presence because you sing or pray or read - he will manifest his presence because of who you are which subsequently leads to what you do. The real cosmic battle is not out there it is inside of you, in your inner space. We should wage war against pride, against rebellion, against indifference, against unbelief, against a casual indifference to our own sin, against our unwillingness to keep the Royal law.

What are we denying ourselves by refusing to let go of certain things?

Once the eyes of our hearts are opened we gain access to understanding both the universe within as well as the universe without. Outside of God we will not have balance our pursuit of understanding one will cause us to neglect and misunderstand the other.

"That you might know the hope to which he has called you, his glorious inheritance in

the saints and his incomparable power for us who believe"

What is your point of view? Think about these words again "**point of view**", because what you see is determined by what you are looking out from. We must press in to God until we can see through the eyes of our hearts.

> See Isaiah 55:8-9, *"For my thoughts are not your thoughts, neither are your ways my ways declares the Lord. As the heavens are higher than the earth so are my ways higher than your ways and my thoughts than your thoughts."*

As high as the heavens are above the earth that's a long way. So is it possible to understand God except through the eyes of the heart? The eyes of the heart interpret for the spirit; the natural eyes interpret for the soul. The soul is restored and our inner space is conquered by God when we draw close enough to interpret through the eyes *(understanding)* of the heart. God is often further than the physical eyes can see, making it an impossibility to understand what he is doing apart from faith.

The one key that gives access to all other keys is of course the Royal Law - love at God's intended level.

Can we give him sufficient of our inner space so that we can love at his level.

> *"I am the true vine, and my Father is the gardener. He cuts off every branch in me that bears no fruit, while every branch that does bear fruit he prunes so that it will be*

even more fruitful. You are already clean because of the word I have spoken to you. Remain in me and I will remain in you. No branch can bare fruit by itself; it must remain in the vine. Neither can you bare fruit unless you remain in me. I am the vine you are the branches. I any man remains in me and I in him, he will bare much fruit; apart from me you can do nothing. If anyone does not remain in me he is like a branch that is thrown away and withers, such branches are picked up throw into the fire and burned. If you remain in me and my words remain in you, ask whatever you wish and it will be given you This is to my Fathers glory that you bear much fruit showing yourself to be my disciple. As the Father has loved, so have I loved you. Now remain in my love." John 15:1-9

How do we remain in him? By remaining in his love! *"If you obey my commands you will remain in my love, just as I have obeyed my Fathers commands and remain in his love."* John 15:10

There is another way of dealing with whatever you are dealing with now. Why be limited by the boundaries of the third dimension when you have access to the fourth dimension?

Our time and energy should be given over to the cultivation of love at his level.

The greater we love at God's intended level the greater our lights will brighten.

> *"I have told you this so that my joy may be in you and so that your joy may be complete. My command is this, love each other as I have loved you. Greater love has no-one than this that he lay down his life for his friends. You are my friends if you do what I command."* John 15:11

Love increases power and power brightens the light.

He died for you so that you would **love** for him. Will you pause for a moment just to realise how much God loves people. This life is a rehearsal for the real thing which lasts forever. Aren't you glad you have made it to the real thing!

> *"I no longer call you servants because a servant does not know his master's business. Instead I have called you friends, for everything that I learned from my Father I have made known to you. You did not choose me, but I chose you and appointed you to go and bear fruit - fruit that will last. Then the Father will give you everything (whatever) you ask in my name. This is my command, love each other."* John 15:15

If you do this one thing, you can ask and receive anything. If you don't do this one thing and what you get will be limited.

Listen..... *MAN CANNOT LIVE BY BREAD ALONE*

Chapter 13

ON AND IN
THROUGH OBEDIENCE

It is time now to take a leap forward. Now that you have had a reminder or first time revelation of the importance of the commands to love at God's level it is time to press on and establish yourself in the Promised Land.

We have learned that the foundation of the Royal Law - appropriating faith which leads to obedience - is the key that releases heaven's blessings into the earth's atmosphere.

> The Israelites had wandered in the wilderness for 40 years on their way from Egypt to Caanan - the Promised Land. The journey could have taken a mere two weeks. The reason for this delay is found in verse 6 of Joshua 15
>
> *"The Israelites had moved about in the desert forty years until all the men who were*

of military age when they left Egypt had died, since they had not obeyed the LORD. For the LORD had sworn to them that they would not see the land that he had solemnly promised their fathers to give us, a land flowing with milk and honey."

In reading the history of these 40 years two things emerge:

The Israelites did not obey God's word.
The Israelites feared to go in and invade the land.

We might say, fear and unbelief led to disobedience!

The three obstacles to advancing are always: sin, fear or doubt.

They **underestimated** God's ability.

Out of all the Israelites who were set free from Egypt, only two men actually went on to live in the Promised Land, namely: Joshua and Caleb.

All of them were set free under the same terms but only two found out that the promises of God were true - thousands upon thousands missed out on promised-land living. They missed out because they were judging things through natural reasoning rather than by faith.

Joshua and Caleb were among twelve spies

(representatives) sent in to spy out the Promised Land. Only these two men said that the land could be taken, even though God had promised the land to them.

Fear that the promises of God are not true is the snare that leads to disobedience which in turn leads to missing out on living in the Promised Land.

God acts when we obey his word - obedience unlocks and activates the promises.

The tragedy is that the thousands upon thousands who did not enter could have done so if only they would have trusted God's word.

Faith is not a product of the reasoning faculties!

We are about to understand what they would have seen *(manifest)* if only they had obeyed God's word. Remember, they greatly feared the Canaanites who lived in the Promised Land. This fear of obeying God due to reasoning rather than standing on the promises of God's word would cost them beyond measure. They had not understood how God would do it so they reasoned that he wouldn't or couldn't. Read that important line again.

Their first task *(a major one)* was to cross the River Jordan but they had not reckoned on the following:

> Joshua 4:23, *"For the LORD your God dried up the Jordan before you until you had*

crossed over. The LORD your God did to the Jordan just what he had done to the Red Sea when he dried it up before us until we had crossed over."

You would think that the Israelites would have trusted God due to what he had done in the past. He had dried up the Red Sea - could he not now then, dry up the River Jordan?

They had seen how supernaturally he works to fulfill his word and carry out his promises when his word is obeyed. *"Moses lift up your staff..."*

When God repeated his miracle by drying up the Jordan look what happened to the thing the Israelites feared, namely: The Amorites and Canaanites?

Joshua 5:1, *"Now when all the Amorite kings west of the Jordan and all the Canaanite kings along the coast heard how the LORD had dried up the Jordan before the Israelites until we had crossed over, their hearts melted and they no longer had the courage to face the Israelites."*

The battle belongs to the Lord!

Remember, God doesn't usually use bridges, often his promises are fulfilled through supernatural means. This is how God dealt with the thing they fear. It was God who took care of the enemy and not the people. He was simply looking for obedience. And when he comes will he find a people who have enough faith to love at his intended level?

God knew that they had no need to fear because he knows the future. He simply asks us to trust and obey his word to us. He will keep his word but until you understand and are rooted and established in love Satan will always be able to get in and cause you to doubt or misinterpret the goodness of God's word as it pertains to you. If you are walking in the awareness of incredibly good news it will become obvious to all that you are.

When we obey his word he removes the obstacles.

Having entered the land and knowing that their enemies no longer had the courage to face them you would have thought that they would have rampaged through, taking the land but God had different ideas in v2 he told Joshua,

> *"Make flint knives and circumcise the Israelites again. So Joshua made flint knives and circumcised the Israelites at Gibeath Haaraloth."*

> And in v 4, *"Now this is why he did so: All those who came out of Egypt—all the men of military age—died in the desert on the way after leaving Egypt. "*

The rite of circumcision marked Israel's position as God's covenant people. When God made the original covenant with Abraham, he required that each male would be circumcised as a sign of cutting off the old life and beginning the new. The ones who didn't enter the Promised Land were in Covenant with God, the promises were theirs, yet, they failed to unlock the promises through their **disobedience.** It was indeed a tragedy but God's plan wasn't thwarted, he simply raised up the next generation. He will always do what he has promised to do, yet, tragically so many of his people miss out on what he has promised to do because of lack of obedience.

God gives the sign of the Covenant to the next generation. They are circumcised and then they celebrate the Passover for the first time in a long time and only the third time in 40 years.

> *"On the evening of the fourteenth day of the month, while camped at Gilgal on the plains of the Jericho the Israelites celebrated the Passover."*

Isn't it strange that the Israelites invaded Canaan set up camp two miles from Jericho and were then told by God to stop, circumcise the men then celebrate the Passover?

The principle is this: **when we obey God he brings about the victory.** Stand firm and see your deliverance. Trust, follow and obey.

v11 *"the day after the Passover, that very day, they ate some of the produce of the land: unleavened bread and roasted grain."*

What is the significance of this? Well God had promised, the Promised Land to the Israelites - a land that would be bountiful.

Remember, they had been in the desert for 40 years and God had miraculously supplied Manna to the hungry Israelites. In the beautiful Promised Land they no longer needed this food supply because the Promised Land was ready for harvesting and planting.

It was just has he had promised!

We can enter our own promised land by trusting and obeying God.

We have his promises.

Those who did not enter due to fear resulting in disobedience could not foresee the following:

God had promised therefore, God was in control of the situation. **"Circumcise the men then celebrate the Passover."** They had feared the natural circumstances so much that they could not trust the word of God. So they did not enter...

However, for those who did enter, this is what they experienced.

Joshua 5:13 -6:6, *"Now when Joshua was near Jericho, he looked up and saw a man standing in front of him with a drawn sword in his hand. Joshua went up to him and asked, "Are you for us or for our enemies?" "Neither," he replied, "but as commander of the army of the LORD I have now come." Then Joshua fell facedown to the ground in reverence, and asked him, "What message does my Lord have for his servant? The commander of the Lord's army replied, "Take off your sandals, for the place where you are standing is holy." And Joshua did so. Now Jericho was tightly shut up because of the Israelites. No one went out and no one came in. Then the LORD said to Joshua, "See, I have delivered Jericho into your hands, along with its king and its fighting men. March around the city once with all the armed men. Do this for six days. Have seven priests carry trumpets of rams' horns in front of the ark. On the seventh day, march around the city seven times, with the priests blowing the trumpets. When you hear them sound a long blast on the trumpets, have all the people give a loud shout; then the wall of the city will collapse and the people will go up, every man straight in."*

You can enter your promised land because obedience is something you can carry out. Most people can't obey God because they can't trust implicitly the outcome. My advice to you today is, 'remove the doubt' by fulfilling the Royal Law. This alone will give you unending confidence to trust God. It is my belief that we are living in the synergy of the ages. In a recent prayer meeting I heard God say the following, 'you are standing on the edge of a million answered prayers.' Is this something that you can believe? If so don't miss out begin to put into practice the principles revealed in this book for you have not yet become all that you are.

> *"So Joshua son of Nun called the priests and said to them, 'Take up the ark of the covenant of the LORD and have seven priests carry trumpets in front of it.' Then the Lord said to Joshua, 'See I have delivered Jericho into your hands along with its king and fighting men'."*

Joshua was, faithful, he trusted God and obeyed his word. His example has touched millions of lives. The price of ill discipline is far greater than the price paid for discipline. The momentary pain of discipline and obedience can have eternal gain. We are to obey God and reason that he will work supernaturally to achieve for us what he has promised. If need be, God will, at the right time, create a miracle to accompany our obedience. God is outside of natural law and is not therefore restricted by it. He can literally do anything and anyway he desires.

The lesson to learn is: do not fear because you cannot see how God is going to do it. I repeat, God is not restricted by natural law, he can and will do what he has promised either conventionally or unconventionally.

Chapter 14

CHOICES

The time has come for you to make some choices. Are you ready?

There is immense power in decision. If you truly make a decision in God he will back it with his power.

The choices are we either have now and pay the price now in order to have what we desire or we have now and pay the price later. Thus, Credit cards should be renamed Debt cards.

When King David went to fight Goliath the narrative says that he left his baggage behind and went to slay Goliath. We can see some wonderful spiritual truth when we compare this episode with what happened in the life of David's predecessor King Saul. In relation to my own life I carried unnecessary baggage into the ministry and all the way to the mission field. What a waste of energy it is to carry such weight!

In the following Scripture verses we find that Saul is hiding himself among the baggage,

> 1 Samuel 10:22, *"So they enquired further of the Lord, 'has the man come here yet?' And the Lord said, 'Yes, he has hidden himself amongst the baggage.'*

The point of what I am saying is this: if we hide amongst the baggage we will eventually return to what is in the baggage:

Our own means
Sinful habits
Independence
Prideful thinking
Physical attributes
Personality

We are to be cleansed of our sin then purged of our self.

We see in the narrative that Saul began again to rely on his own means, in the absence of the prophet Samuel he makes a sacrifice to God, knowing that only the prophet should do this. The result was that God decided to replace Saul with David whom he described as a man after his own heart. It is more comfortable to hide among the baggage than it is to leave it behind and trust only in God for tomorrow. The reason for this is that we have always trusted what is contained in the baggage.

Saul was hiding among the baggage and we see that God eventually showed the people where Saul was hiding. The truth is we can generally see what is wrong with one another and that is why we discuss one another's faults but because we have not learned to, 'speak the truth in love' it doesn't come into the open. This is why we need to have accountability and this is formed through discipleship based on relationships.

What baggage would you have others who affect your life to put down. What irritates you?

What about your spouse – if you could change them in any area and it was in their power to change what would you ask them to change? What about your parents? What about friends? What about your church?

Well God is our best friend and understanding human nature as he does – he goes to great lengths, in his word, to tell us what we need to change.

How the baggage limits us!

Get someone to carry a heavy bag – then to carry a bag with nothing in it. The difference will determine a lot, like, how far the person can go and in what manner they go.

We hide among the baggage because we assume that everything we need is in the bag so we walk around with all kinds of excess weight weighing us down.

God wants you to know what and where you are going to and he wants you to do it without your baggage.

Bible teacher Ed Cole once commented that Winners focus on what they are going to, whilst losers focus on what they are going through. Peter walked on the water just as long as he focused on what he was going to. As soon as he didn't he sank! Get in the centre of God's will for being in the centre of God's will is infinitely better than anything the world has to offer. It should be us, meaning me and you, who set the agenda in the places that we live and not the Devil.

> Revelation 4:1 says, *"After this I looked and there before me was a door standing open in heaven. And the voice I had first heard speaking to me like a trumpet said, 'Come up here, and I will show you what must take place after this."*

instead of relying on your baggage start to knock on God's door.

> *"For everyone who asks receives; he who seeks finds; and to him who knocks, the door will be opened."* Matthew 7:8

 Put off the old garments and clothe yourself with a new wardrobe.

"Be transformed by the renewing of your mind". Romans 12:3

You will never be able to hear God clearly in a particular area until he has renewed your mind. It is time to do all that we can to be transformed in our thinking. Every physical reality began its life as a thought. The building you are in began its life as an idea. The park that you walk in, the road you drive on…

The author Victor Hugo said this about ideas,

'An invasion of armies can be resisted, but not an idea whose time has come.'

We must continue to lay down our baggage and in particular the baggage of wrong thinking that we have been both convinced and deceived into believing is right thinking.

> Matthew 7:12, *"So in everything do to others what you would have them do to you, for this sums up the Law and the Prophets."*

Sum means total of adding everything up. This is what they were trying to put over in all of the Law and what the Prophets were saying, throughout Scripture.

Do is an active word it means start to do something for others. Because of our worth God wants us to be treated like his children and that is best achieved when we his children grasp this and implement it on behalf of others. Do something unexpected for a person who you think doesn't deserve it – something you would dearly love them to do for you.

The price that was paid for you and me is evidence of how much we are worth to God. This fact ought to tell us something. We must narrow the 'world' of John 3:16 to the individual,

> *"For God so loved John Bullock that he gave his only begotten Son that if John believes in him he shall not perish but have eternal life."*

That is the price…

> In Matthew 6:27-29 we read, *"Who by worrying can add a single hour to his life? And why do you worry about clothes? See how the lilies of the field grow. They do not labour or spin. Yet I tell you that not even Solomon in all his splendour was dressed like one of these."*

The key to waiting through any situation is to trust, follow and obey. This process is the absolute opposite and antithesis of being governed by feelings and natural circumstances! Like never before you are ready to allow

God to go much deeper within you. Here's how…

ALLOWING GOD TO TAKE THE INNER SPACE

So much research has gone into trying to understand the Universe or *Outer Space* but how much has gone into trying to understand *Inner Space* what makes us human beings tick from the inside?

It is my belief that the way we see our environment on the outside can be completely transformed if we change the environment on the inside. Don't allow the paradigm *(idea or concept)* that you live under to make your understanding of reality redundant.

Remember the point I made earlier:

All the knowledge, understanding and experience gathered in life can only be absorbed into the foundation of what we are in essence. Right foundations, therefore, are imperative. The Scripture tells us that we must be <u>rooted</u> and <u>established</u> in love.

Coming to Christ gives us an opportunity to re-establish our foundations. However, it is likely that you have never properly done this.

> Deuteronomy 30:11-14, *"Now what I am commanding you today is not too difficult for you today or beyond your reach. It is not*

up in heaven, so that you have to ask, who
will ascend into heaven to get it and
proclaim it to us so that we may obey it?
Nor is it beyond the sea, so that you have to
ask, who will cross the sea to get it and
proclaim it to us so that we may obey it?
No, the word is very near you; it is in your
mouth and in your heart so that you may
obey it."

The enemy is waging psychological warfare against the body of Christ constantly undermining us and holding us in the prison of OUR MEMORIES and the limitations of strongholds. We are to be changed from glory to glory and this means allowing God into every area of our lives.

All forms of created life are based on **cells.** Cells are the building blocks of the human body, plants, animals, and every other living thing. The human body, which in itself is an engineering wonder, contains about 100,000,000,000,000 cells *(can you comprehend that number?)* of which there are a vast variety. In his wisdom, he designated these cells to perform specific tasks. They grow, multiply, and eventually die - right on schedule.

Though they are invisible to the naked eye, cells are not the smallest particle known to man. Cells consist of numerous tinier structures called molecules, which are comprised of even smaller structures called **elements** and within elements can be found even tinier structures called

atoms. Atoms are so small that a full stop contains more than a billion of them. Yet an atom is made up almost entirely of empty space. The remainder of the atom is composed of **protons, neutrons,** and **electrons.** Protons and neutrons are clustered together in a minuscule and extremely dense nucleus at the very centre of the atom. Little bundles of energy called electrons whiz around this nucleus at the speed of light. These core building blocks hold all things together.

Having understood those basic elements of life we need to know that these elements work to order and even to some routine. Scientists call this atomic energy. This scientific term describes what they can't explain. A key to our understanding of life and its origins in the broader sense is: where does the atom get its energy? And by what force is it held together?

We must go to God's word for our answers. Hebrews 1:3 tells us,

"He is sustaining all things by the power of his word." and Col.1:17 reminds us that, *"in him all things hold together."*

God is the glue, the life-force that holds the whole of life together. So often we look at this Scripture in terms of our world out there – rather than our world within.

Now this amazing journey inside us is only part of the

picture - this is an explanation of the physics of what makes man and it is extraordinary. But what about the Inner Space of our character, personality and temperament? This is the mind, the will and the emotions the things that make up our souls. The soul is the part of us that relates to our natural world that surrounds us but the spirit is the thing that transforms our characters by governing our souls. Until you come to Christ your soul is rampant in its control over you.

The mind, the will and the emotions are governed entirely by your environs dictating the ongoing formation of your character, personality and temperament. It is obvious from our understanding of scripture that the well-being of the natural elements can be greatly affected by the state of the spiritual.

How far have we allowed the Spirit to transform us?

> *"Do not conform any longer to the patterns of this world, but be transformed (metamorphosis) by the renewing of your mind."* Romans 12:2

A great key in determining whether you will reach your potential in God or not *and* that is no light thing can be found in two words - **CONFORMED** *or* **TRANSFORMED**. Are you **conformed** to the pattern of this world or are you

transformed by the renewing of your mind. My observations and personal experience lead me to believe that not many believers have been transformed. Whoever you are, whatever your background, whatever you have done, you must be transformed out of your natural culture and traditions into the culture of the Kingdom of God.

The door is grace. The provision is the Holy Spirit and the means is the renewing of the mind. The real cosmic battle is not in Outer Space but rather in Inner Space. In terms of Outer Space - the Bible tells us what is out there. It is not a mystery!

> Eph.6:10, *"For our struggle is not against flesh and blood but against the rulers, against the authorities, against the powers of this dark world and against the spiritual forces of evil in the heavenly realm. Therefore, put on the full armour of God so that when the day of evil comes, you may be able to stand your ground..."*

Now look at this again - you may be able to stand your ground. The Devil can only attack the ground that you are stood on - you have taken it from him! So how do we fight this cosmic war? Well it is not with nuclear bombs or guided missiles. No God has devised another way. You take this ground in accordance with the ground you have allowed God to posses in you. Wow!

What is the armour of God?

Quite simply it is the truth we have applied to our lives in a given area.

> *Then: 2 Corinthians 10:4,"For though we live in the world, we do not wage war as the world does. The weapons we fight with are not the weapons of the world. On the contrary, they have divine power to demolish strongholds. We demolish arguments and every pretension that sets itself up against the knowledge of God, and we take captive every thought to make it obedient to Christ. And we will be ready to punish every act of disobedience, once your obedience is complete."*

Real spiritual victory is linked to obedience to God's word. Look at the link to this in the passage we looked at in

> *Rom. 12: 2, "Do not conform any longer to the patterns of this world, but be transformed (metamorphosis) by the renewing of your mind. Then you will be able to test and approve God's good, perfect and pleasing will for your lives."*

If you can allow God to conquer the Inner Space you will see how easy it is to conquer the Outer Space.

We can only conquer the one by allowing God to conquer the other. We must allow him to transform us through the renewing of our minds. The main things that need to be understood about man and his world can't be taught in Universities because they don't come through knowledge - they come through wisdom that is imparted through revelation from the creator and the sustainer of the universe.

Charisma that has its source in the Spirit and flows through character is God's intention. However, there is another kind of charisma it has its roots in the soul and flows through personality.

The latter has to maintain and build by using manipulation through personality and rather than operate in the real anointing that affects the spirit it operates on hype which affects only the soul! To the immature, both kinds of charisma appear to be the same. My heart's cry is not one of criticism but desperation; surely we have had enough of the charisma that is born in the soul of man? If we will cultivate our hearts and make it the goal of our lives to fulfil the Royal Law then we will allow God to take our inner space. As he takes our inner space we will in him begin to take the outer space that consists of what is going on on the outside of us.

Begin your revolution…..now!
> **"Trust in the LORD with all your heart and lean not on your own understanding."**
> Proverbs 3:5-6

Are you restrained by the Royal Law?

Belief is in the integrity of God's word. If God speaks then we can stand on what he says by faith. However, you cannot speak to a mountain and then interpret the result through sense knowledge. Truth is based on the fact that God does not lie, therefore, his word is true. If his word is true therein lays all the evidence that we need in interpreting reality.

God's word has to be taken seriously. If God says, 'I command you to love at this level then we simply must take him seriously because there will be dramatic consequences if we don't. The Royal Law is to become the restraining influence on our lives. The reason for this is that the keeping of God's commands to love gives us access to obtaining the keys of the kingdom. Not every believer gets the keys of the kingdom. Of course they are potentially in the hands of every believer but they are linked to our obedience!

We have not fully realised who we are in Christ or what we have in him. When we do everything changes - we realise that God and not the world is our best chance of success, prosperity, peace, joy and fulfilment.

The stipulation placed upon God's word is not experience it and it will come true it is **believe** it and it will come to pass. The thing that pleases God most is when we recognise the integrity of God's word and refuse to pass it through the sieve of sense knowledge - we cannot, simply cannot, interpret God through the means of feelings or circumstances.

God asks us to believe him. Interpretation of facts through sense knowledge belongs to this world because the senses were given so that we could understand our world and thus enlighten the soul. God has not subjected knowledge of himself to the same means - not at all. He communicates through revelation knowledge. Things that are revealed to us by way of the spirit and the ingredient that allows this to function is, *"Faith expressing itself through love."* hence the seriousness of the commands to love at God's level. As we approached the month of November 2002 I was about to be tested in this.

Chapter 15

DAVID

The last time I had seen him he had put on weight and was exaggerating his stomach as my brother Kevin and I badgered him with regard to the weight gain. As we have moved on to maturity it is a subject that often crops up when we brothers get together. Kevin, the eldest, leads the field at the moment. The truth is, in our younger days, we were all athletes, not carrying an ounce of fat between us. Those days were long gone and much lamented.

The phone rang interrupting a nice social evening we were enjoying with our friends Rueben and Marilyn Jenkins. It was my younger brother Ian sounding alarmed and eager for help, 'Its our David' he said 'he's admitted that he is a cocaine addict and feels that some people are after him and want him out of the way.' he went on to tell me that a desperate David was at my parents home and come what may he was leaving town that night. 'I'll phone you back in a few minutes' I murmured trying to gather my thoughts. After a brief chat with Deb we agreed that David should come down to stay with us, We arranged to meet up in Birmingham - my dad bringing David and Rueben travelling up with me. A few minutes later we were on our way to the rendezvous.

It was a moment that I will never forget when David walked into the service station restaurant he had not had a drug for two days and was evidently in the throes of going 'Cold Turkey' He had shed almost four stone in weight and was looking gaunt and frightened, He looked like my late uncle Tom who had been interned in a prison of war camp at the hands of the Japanese in World War Two. It was the ears that did it - pronounced as they stuck out of the side of a face that had shrunken due to malnutrition. The enemy of our souls having the same affect as that of the Japanese soldiers who tormented our prisoners of war.

We said little - everybody present knowing the score. Given the circumstances any attempt at making polite conversion seemed to be a mockery. The scene and mood was dampened further by some unruly looking sorts who were travelling on after a Manchester United game. After a quick coffee, Rueben, David and I headed back to the Rhondda Valleys.

David had travelled light to say the least - he was penniless and had with him only the clothes that he was wearing. Once we arrived home I fed him and chatted briefly - not wanting to put any pressure on him - before we went to bed, my first instinct was to make him feel as secure as possible. It was six thirty in the morning.

The next day Kipper as he has been affectionately known since childhood came down at tea-time, it was the first sleep and decent food he'd had in days. He'd been making his own way in a flat but had been surviving on the odd bowl of cornflakes as cocaine had almost completely consumed his life.

He began to tell us just where he had been and what he had been doing. Thus, began the unfolding of his life. He revealed to us that the last few days were the longest he had been without drugs for about twenty years. I was amazed at the depth of his problem. David and I probably hadn't been in each others company for more than one month collectively during those twenty years.

He went on to reveal the kind of people he had been dealing with of late and was clearly out of his league. He was genuinely scared for his life and had hit rock-bottom. I was looking at my own brother shipwrecked and who without the charity of his own flesh and blood would be destitute. It was a very painful experience and my heart was aching that it had come to this. We had not had time to even think things through. It seemed like one minute he was not with us and the next he was, not only was he with us but as he couldn't go back to where the rest of the family live in Blackpool he had nowhere else to go. We had a lodger but such was his plight that he didn't even have a change of underwear let alone any means to look after himself, I looked at him and loved him - this was my brother!

Have you ever lived with another person who is not in your immediate family - we have several times both in Africa and in the UK and it has never been easy. This time the change in our domestic situation had come without warning. What did it mean for Debbie and I and for our kids, Chris *(12)* and Beth *(10)*? For a start we had to realise that there was someone among us who was coming off a long standing drug habit the hard way, unknown territory for sure. Chris and Beth would have to share a bedroom again and Debbie and I would have to make unprecedented adjustments to our lives.

My brother at 40 years of age had no where else to go and because of the situation in Blackpool no one else to turn to. He did not exist as far as the social security people were concerned, was ill due to withdrawal from drugs and had no money at all. We hadn't planned to take on this responsibility and it has to be said, risk, but short of putting him on the streets, we had no choice. The thing that hurt me most was the fact that he was absolutely destitute and was at the mercy of kindness and charity, albeit the kindness and mercy of his own brother.

As he described some recent beatings he had taken where he was not able to defend himself because of a problem he had with his shoulders dislocating, I almost felt the pain for him. On one occasion when I was alone pondering his plight I sobbed as the hurt I was feeling for him poured out. Of course, I knew that it was self-inflicted and that he had done a lot of bad things but I had grown up with him when he was a fresh-faced kid often living awkwardly in the shadow of his two older brothers Kevin, and myself.

I had known little of his life since I left Blackpool to go to Bible College in 1987. However, over the next few days the years that had separated us - geographically at least - were put to one side and we became friends. More than that I began to see a wonderful principle: once a person comes into the environment of God's love he regains his rights. David still had no means to support himself but his needs would be met because, no matter what he had done, he was a legitimate candidate to receive God's love, including provision from those who love God.

I had told him on the night I picked him up,' you are entering my world now, please don't bring your world into my world.' I knew with confidence that he would like the world that I lived in - I wanted him to see life at first hand in a Christian family, imperfections and all but more than anything I wanted him to walk in dignity. I wanted him to know that this could be a beginning not the end that he had recently contemplated through suicide.

Debbie and I started to fill his life with encouragement and surround him with love, at the same time making a conscious effort to feed him up. The banter began again that his slight frame *(he is 6ft 2in)* would son be carrying more unneeded flesh than mine was. We did a lot of laughing as we reminisced our younger years in Bradford and Blackpool.

He was doing well coming off a two ounce a day cocaine habit but at times his mood would dip as hopelessness reared its ugly nature. In human terms his plight was not good. At nights he was sweating profusely particularly as he was suffering nightmares during the breaks in the insomnia that was plaguing him. Above all, he had no future, a temporary resident of charity but what then? He came to us on Tuesday and on Saturday I informed him with a wink that it was a rule of our household that everyone goes to church on Sundays. In fact, he came readily.

I was preaching at my unsaved brother who needed to find God's grace and mercy as much as anyone who had ever sat under my ministry. Up to this point, we had purposely tried to show God to David rather than preach at him.

As I began my sermon I felt that God was urging me not to pull any punches and encouraging me that if I would say what he wanted me to say despite my audience then he would back-up what I said. I went for it and preached a very strong message - not particularly gospel. At the end I made a pointed appeal for salvation, asking people who were responding to signify by raising their hand. There was a pregnant pause before a solitary hand began to rise - it was David! Was this really happening? David had never visited us in the Rhondda before, let alone come to church.

'David come out here would you?' I said as tears began to well up in my eyes. I knew the battle had been won - he was the Lords! David humbly came to the front as the congregation looked on in amazement. I gave him a hug and then asked one of our elders to come and pray for the new child of God. After this many people cried out like never before for members of their own family.

On returning home we phoned Blackpool and gave our believing Mother the news that she had prayed for 18 years son number three was in the Kingdom of God. Salvation is real and it lasts forever.

Chapter 16

PROOF OF LIFE

How we see ourselves will determine how we imagine others will see us and ultimately how they will see us.

> *"They said, 'The land we explored devours those living in it. All the people we saw there are of great size. We saw the Nephilim there (the descendants of Anak come from the Nephilim). We seemed like grasshoppers in our own eyes, and we looked the same to them.'"*

The Principle of the Veil

> *"But their minds were made dull, for to this day the same veil remains when the old covenant is read. It has not been removed, because only in Christ is it taken away. Even to this day when Moses is read, a veil covers their hearts. But whenever anyone turns to the Lord, the veil is taken away."*

The principle we can learn from this is that 'people can only see as far as the veil allows them to see. In the case of the Israelites they could *(can)* only see as far as the Old Covenant allows them to see.

The same principle can be seen in terms of non-believers.

> *"And even if our gospel is veiled, it is veiled to those who are perishing. The god of this age has blinded the minds of unbelievers, so that they cannot see the light of the gospel of the glory of Christ, who is the image of God"*
> 2 Corinthians 4:3-4

The devil knows that, 'What we SEE will pre-determine what we will BE!'

Jackie Pullinger said, 'What is the world's wealth, if you have seen him?'

See Him!
See Ourselves!
See our world around us!

'Don't pray for what you should do in the midst of a dying people.' 'When you see them with his eyes go to them with his heart.' Compassion is not an emotion it is an action.' We must do what is necessary to go on seeing with His eyes. There is a great difference between an act of religion and an act of the heart, even if they appear to be the same. The heart will cause us to sacrifice so that we can advance the Kingdom of God.

We need to change our mindset and see these things as immense positives rather than negatives. There are results to our actions. Proof of life is a term used by those dealing with kidnappers. The kidnappers have to prove that the victims are still alive.

Our task is to prove that Jesus Christ is still alive. God's word is clear on how we should do this, 'He promises if you do this, then I shall do that on your behalf.

God is saying prove me in this. It is time to pursue the Lord until we can see further than we have yet seen.

Twelve spies entered the land but only two truly saw. Joshua and Caleb were the only two who were determined to pursue until they could SEE. Who today will arm themselves with the same attitude?

It is high time that we stopped accepting partial victory. We must put the enemy to death in a given area.

The Word of the Lord is, It is time to update your testimony. It is time to remove the veil so that you can see beyond what you have seen.

Chapter 17

CLIMBING JACOB'S LADDER

Jacob 28:10:17, *"Jacob left Beersheba and set out for Haran. When he reached a certain place, he stopped for the night because the sun had set. Taking one of the stones there, he put it under his head and lay down to sleep. He had a dream in which he saw a stairway resting on the earth, with its top reaching to heaven, and the angels of God were ascending and descending on it. There above it stood the Lord, and he said, I am the lord, the God of your Father Abraham and the God of Isaac. I will give you and your descendants the land on which you are lying. Your descendants will be like the dust of the earth, and you will spread out to the west and to the east, to the north and to the south. All peoples on earth will be blessed through you and your offspring. I am with you and will watch over you wherever you go, and I will bring you back to this land. I*

*will not leave you until I have done what I
have promised you."*

If we are going to have authority on earth we need to have earthly representation in heaven. What I mean by this is apostolic ministry!

The difference between pastoral ministry and apostolic ministry is pastoral ministry **manages** and apostolic ministry **advances.**

Of course we need both but we must realise that pastoral ministry alone will not bring about the necessary change – the truth is that many communities have gone too far to be restored by pastoral ministry alone. We must have a people who will pay the price to climb the ladder into the heavenly realms.

Once this advantage has been gained we can then see the battle on earth from an earthly perspective. This allows us to see what the enemy is doing to the church and to individuals.

However, it may seem at times we are not wrestling against flesh and blood.

> *"For we are not wrestling against flesh and
> blood but spiritual forces of darkness in the
> heavenly realms."*

The church has to send an advance party into the heavenly realms so that we can understand the battle that is taking place in the earth's atmosphere.

THE ANSWER IS WRITTEN IN THE SKY

In Romans 11:33-36 we are told the following, *"Oh the depth of the riches of the wisdom and knowledge of God! How unsearchable his judgements, and his paths beyond tracing out! Who has known the mind of the Lord? Or who has been his counsellor? Who has ever given to God, that God should repay him? For from him and through him and to him are all things. To him be the glory forever and ever! Amen."*

And in Isaiah 55:9

"As the heavens are higher than the earth, so are my ways higher than your ways and my thoughts than your thoughts."

In Bruce Porter's "The Martyrs Torch" he quotes the Scientists as saying,

'I can say with some confidence that the heavens are indeed quite a bit higher than the earth. In fact the very nearest star we observe is Alpha Centauri C *(Proxima)* which is about 4.2 light-years away! That means it takes more than four years for light o reach us from that star, travelling at approximately 186,000 miles per second! The Milky Way our home galaxy, of which our solar system is a part, is about 100,000 light years across and contains several hundreds of billions of stars of various sizes and colours like our sun.

Beyond our home galaxy, our nearest galactic neighbour is M-31, or the Great Andromeda Galaxy. It's the most distant object that we can see with the naked eye, about 2 million light-years distant. Beyond this are many hundreds of billions of huge galaxies, each containing hundreds of billions of stars. Then there are billions more of huge clusters of galaxies, and beyond them are clusters of clusters of galaxies that form gigantic walls of galaxies... Whew!

> Based upon Isaiah 55:9, *"As the heavens are higher than the earth, so are my ways higher than your ways and my thoughts than your thoughts."*

Bruce said,

'I think the Lord is trying to tell us that, compared to him; we are somewhat cerebrally challenged *(to put it politely)*.'

When we try to comprehend the workings and purposes of God, we invariably make the mistake of putting him in boxes that make him more manageable in our own understanding.'

We should ask the question what experiences and traditions have led us to our present understanding and levels of expectation.

How big is the God who dwells within us?

The following prophecy was given to me in January 2002

> *What we feel and see is very significant; however, what is behind what we see is amazing. The depth of the starry host is beyond human comprehension. In order to achieve what I have planned you must go beyond what you see and take others beyond what they see. All things are hidden in me - your healing, deliverance, revival, revolution...but these things are only available and become real as you learn to see what is behind what you see. As you go further than what you feel - as you dwell in superiority to sense knowledge. Behind what you see is a long chain of grace, mercy and compassion accompanied by mounting unwrapped gifts. And everything is shadowed by my power which leads to invested authority.*

Apostolic ministry is reaching high enough to do what man can't do. We have to have hope when only a supernatural answer will do.

The Bible says that Jesus has ascended to fill the whole universe. 'Lord help us to understand what you have invested in us in order to keep us from sin and sustain us in authority'. We walk by faith and not by sight! Faith sees further than sight; faith can look beyond the sky and see, in the spirit a world that is the parent world of our world. It is time to change dimension.

Chapter 18

LIFE IN A NEW DIMENSION

The Bible tells us this astonishing fact in the book of (*Hebrews 13:8*), *"Jesus Christ is the same yesterday, today and forever."*

Ponder that thought, and consider that you may need to climb to that new dimension.

The third dimensional viewpoint **includes** a scientific analysis of our world but **excludes** the role of the spirit realm.

For the sake of understanding the difference between three dimensions and four look at it this way. In simple terms, the third dimension is that which we see, touch and understand whereas the fourth dimension includes all of that plus an understanding of the spiritual that is behind what we can see, touch and understand.

We must learn to understand life through the **Grid of Scripture.** In other words, it is Scripture that portrays reality so we will only **experience** God and have an understanding of life, to the degree that we believe and practice the truth and reality of Scripture.

If the following was not reality then we would be into the realm of dangerous fantasy

> Matthew. 14:35-36, *"And when the men of that place recognized Jesus, they sent word to all the surrounding country. People brought all their sick to Him and begged Him to let the sick just touch the edge of His cloak, and all who touched Him were healed."*

Why were all the people healed?

Well it had nothing to do with them touching anything physical. There was no magic in His flesh and certainly not in the clothes he wore. Yet, the people were healed as they touched the hem of His garment. In other words it had nothing to do with them touching anything in the third dimension. They were in reality **touching something from the fourth dimension;** something from another world, something from heaven.

Significantly, as they were touched by the fourth dimension the third dimension had to respond. They didn't need bandages or ointment. They were, quite simply, touched by a power that is greater than any power in the third dimension. Not only that, this power is also greater than **all** the powers of darkness.

When Jesus came into our world and conquered the Devil

He opened up the doorway into the Spirit realm, for all people; a doorway that would allow ordinary people to draw from the fourth dimension in order to understand and conquer the obstacles of the third dimension.

He both introduced and showed us how to live with a supernatural element to our lives!

> Jesus said, *"The thief comes only to steal and kill and destroy; I have come that they may have life and have it to the full."* John 10:10

If life to the full is possible, then how foolish it is if we believers do not have life to the full.

Do you want life to the full?

If you do, and I am sure you do, then listen: Jesus seeks to undo all that the enemy has done. And He seeks to do this through His body on earth, the Church. In other words you and me!

> *"The reason the Son of God appeared was to destroy the work of the evil one."* 1 John 3:8

The reason that we human beings cannot understand our world is because we seek to understand it solely through our **rational** and through **science**. The problem is, the fourth dimension will not submit itself to either Science or our human rationale. Personally, I would like to state, 'in answer to scientific dogma, I have become an answer to prayer!'

"Spiritual things are discerned spiritually."

The people, in touching Jesus, were not touching the third dimension they were touching the fourth dimension through the doorway into the fourth dimension, namely: Jesus.

Jesus stood in the gap between our world and the spirit world. The result was the spirit world overruled and corrected the damage that had been done by our fallen world.

This is our inheritance as children of God, if only we will rid ourselves of religious thinking. Even Pentecostal religious thinking and begin to rely on, **'THE ANOINTING'**. And the anointing accompanies our obedience to love!

Jesus had emptied himself of all but the anointing. That is why He said,

> *"Anyone who has faith in me will do what I have been doing. He will do even greater things than these, because I am going to the Father."* John 14:12

The reason for this is quite simple these things happen on our earth due to the anointing and only due to the anointing.

The potential for walking in the anointing is resident in every Spirit filled believer but it is not automatic.

The Apostle Paul said these incredible words in

Romans. 8:10-11, *"But if Christ is in you, your body is dead because of sin, yet your spirit is alive because of righteousness. And if the Spirit of him who raised Jesus from the dead is living in you, He who raised Jesus from the dead will also give life to your mortal bodies through His Spirit who lives in you."*

Realise today, if not before, you have the same spirit living in you as the one who raised Jesus from the dead.

Don't miss this! Listen to these words again.

"And if the Spirit of Him who raised Jesus from the dead is living in you...."

The Spirit of whom?

When we realise this is it any wonder that from time to time believers have even raised the dead, if the same Spirit that raised Jesus is in us. Wow!

"It is not by might or by power, but by my Spirit, says the Lord Almighty." (*Zechariah 4:6*)

If it is the Spirit within us and not the agent that achieves this then surely we should make sure we are filled to capacity with the Holy Spirit. And if it is the same Spirit that was active in Bible days then surely we can expect to see all that happened in the Bible.

Jesus **radiated** the anointing and He has given His body *(The* *church*) His Spirit, so that we have the potential to do exactly the same.

We can do what Jesus did!

We can potentially; but it is not automatic. You see the anointing flows through dead bodies and it will be obstructed to the degree that we allow the old self to live in our bodies. You cannot hold on to sinful actions and attitudes if you want the anointing to flow through you.

You can be touched by the anointing flowing through another person but walking in the anointing is a different matter and is dependent on your obedience to God's word and the leading of the Holy Spirit.

We will only bring the wisdom, power and authority of the fourth dimension to our earth to the degree that we will live as "citizens" of heaven here on earth. For it is the application of heaven's law that leads to heaven's blessing? This book is leading you to make choices; it is choices that unveil the power of decision.

There are no excuses, for God has given His church the ability to break all sin and to be delivered from every demonic foothold. Folks, God can say, **"Be Holy as I am Holy"** because He has given us all that we need to be Holy as He is holy.

We can only do what Jesus did if we will walk as Jesus did. We are all, *"more than conquerors through Christ who strengthens us."*

The religious world cannot understand those who walk in the anointing because the anointing is subject to another world and will not subject itself to methods or the *"traditions of men which nullify the word of God."*

The anointing has its source in God who is not restricted by natural law. Hence we had people touching the life of God through the fleshly body of Jesus. *"All those who touched the hem of His garment were healed."*

There is no doubt in my mind that Smith Wigglesworth's prophecy regarding the end time move of God is correct. He prophesied that the last great move of God would incorporate both the Spirit and the Word.

This is essential to our understanding.

Adherence to the word releases the Spirit!

Real life begins in the Spirit but it then has a **practical outworking** which leads to more Spiritual life being released. So we have a cycle that is initiated by God but partnered by His people, His body on earth. The head always initiates and the body follows. The foundation is love at God's required level and the link is faith which is activated by obedience.

Jesus said, *"I only do what the Father tells me."* This was because,
"Obedience is better than sacrifice."

Whilst **reason** does not usher in the fourth dimension

obedience does. That is why the walls of Jericho fell. Let me give you a startling example of this in the life of Jesus. Remembering that Jesus did only what the father told Him to do.

> Come with me to Mark 8:22-23, *"They came to Bethsaida, and some people brought a blind man and begged Jesus to touch him. He took the blind man by the hand and led him outside. When He had spat on the man's eyes and put His hands on him, Jesus asked, "Do you see anything?"*

Does it actually say, **"Jesus spat on his eyes"**?

The problem is we have assumed that we have understood God and his ways. But listen further.

> John 5:1, *"Jesus gave them this answer: I tell you the truth, the Son can do nothing by Himself; He can do only what he sees his Father doing, because whatever the Father does the Son does."*

God's ways are not our ways but the kingdom advances through God's ways. The body cannot function without the direction of the head.

I repeat, the anointing cannot be contained by methods. God will do it His way through the channel of a Holy people who will sacrifice all to obey him.

This is so that no-one will be in any doubt that it is God acting and not man. Reason does not usher in the **Fourth Dimension**, obedience does. But how can the body obey the head, if the body has only limited communication with the head?

When we come to an understanding of who we are in Christ and the potential that resides within each of us we will increasingly learn to see sin, apathy, indifference and lack of discipline as an enemy. The anointing will flow through you to the degree that you want it to. The answer to the ills of our society is in, "the anointed body of Christ". Folks, it is time to adhere to the word like never before; submit to His Lordship like never before and make contact with heaven like never before. If we love at his level and obey his voice we will do what Jesus did!

The anointing will flow through you to the extent that you are willing to swap your life for His life. We, the existing church must give the lead in changing the mind-set of how people perceive the church. We have our work cut out because many **believers** still see the sweet sentimental little Jesus and have a "hold the fort" mentality. This is not what Jesus intended. He intended us to carry on doing exactly what He did. This is the gospel! We must obey the Father's word so that we can radiate the Spirit and bring the splendour of the fourth dimension into our miserable, sin ridden, satanically controlled planet.

> In our first Scripture in Matthew 14:35 we read, *"And when the men of that place recognised Jesus, they sent word to all the*

195

surrounding country. People brought all their sick to Him and begged him to let the sick just touch the edge of His cloak, and all who touched Him were healed."

Listen now, *"when the men of the place recognised Jesus"*

Our job is to change the mind-set of the people by causing them to recognise that Jesus is living in His church. This can only be achieved in the same way that it always has been achieved. The body moving in the anointing! Soaking, in God, so that we **radiate** his anointing which breaks the yoke of oppression. It is not what we can do but what we allow God to do through us. Give the Spirit precedence over the flesh. Love until we are filled to all the fullness of God and then learn to radiate the life that is within us.

If we are going to change the mindset of our communities we must be prepared to change our own mindset first. Are we prepared?

Revival begins in the church; so if **we don't want it badly enough**, it won't come to our communities. Do we want revival enough to **will** it? Will is directly attached to action.

Chapter 19

IMPREGNATED BY FAITH

God wants to deposit his seed. Our task is to water it until it germinates and grows to its fullness.

> What about this for a powerful Scripture, *"The God who gives life to the dead and calls things that are not as if they were."* Romans.4:17b

This verse is of course speaking of Abraham when his name was changed by God from Abram meaning "Exalted Father" to Abraham meaning "Father of many". Remember Abraham walked around with this name before Isaac was born. When he got to being 100 years of age he was probably a laughing stock. But he was named because of the promise of God that,

> *"All peoples on earth will be blessed through you."* Gen.12:3

God, by changing his name from Abram to Abraham was calling something that was not as if it were. In other words

Abraham was called "father of many" before his firstborn had come into the world. Think about that...

All that we need is the beginning point!

Another example of this was in the life of Noah. God told him to build a boat because the floods were coming. Amazingly Noah spent the next 120 years obeying God. He built the Ark on dry land in a place where it had never rained. Up to that point water had come from the earth.

Noah's lifetime work became his witness. Every time someone asked, 'What is this crazy thing you are doing?' Noah was able to witness of what God had revealed to him. And subsequently warn of God's judgment.

God has always and is always calling things that are not as if they were.

You cannot call something that is as if it is not but you can call something that is not as if it were because, *"Faith is being sure of what you hope for and certain of what you do not see."* It cannot be clearer than that listen again; Faith is **sure** and **certain.**

God calls things that are not yet manifest, in our third dimension *(the natural realm)*, as if they were because they do exist in the fourth dimension *(in the realm of the Spirit)*. And a doorway has been opened between the two realms, "Through Christ". It was He who said, whilst on earth, *"I am the door".*

So, if we can understand that the spirit realm is as real as our material realm and is in fact the parent world of our world i.e. it existed before our world and our world was created out of it. Then faith is believing that God the creator, who is Spirit, can create anything on our behalf in the spirit realm and that this creation can invade our world to meet our needs.

Remember when the sick were healed, as they touched Jesus' garments; they were not healed due to touching anything physical; they were healed due to the fact that they touched the fourth dimension that was radiating through the anointing upon Jesus Christ.

This leads me on to the significance of prayer. When we ask God for something or to act on our behalf the prayer enters the fourth dimension and is heard the moment that we pray it. The answer is then formed in the spirit realm in the fourth dimension and awaits **the proper time** to be answered. This is what we might term the period of incubation. When we do not see before us the answer but we are in reality expectant with it. This is why,

> *"Faith is being sure of what we hope for and certain of what we do not see."* Hebrews 11:1

Note here: **"See"**, *"certain of what we do not see"*. It is in existence even though we cannot see it.

> *"So we fix our eyes not on what is seen but what is unseen".*

How do we fix our eyes on what is unseen? The answer is of course through the principle of faith. By faith we become pregnant with the answer.

Let me explain further. In a human pregnancy the life is created at the point of conception not at the point of birth. So why did God design a nine month term of pregnancy? He did it so that the created life could be fully formed in order that it could be ready to adapt into our world.

If we carry this principle over into the spirit realm we can see something wonderful about faith.

When we pray for something at a personal or church level, this is exactly what happens. God our father hears our prayer straight away. Sometimes He says an outright **no** to our request; sometimes he says an immediate **yes**; but most times he says **wait**.

Now there is a very good reason for this.

God gives the answer immediately but then puts the answer into incubation so that either our world or we, ourselves, can be changed accordingly so that we are ready to receive the answer that has already been formed in the fourth dimension.

The incubation period can be a short or lengthy period, during which time God is preparing things in the third dimension to receive the answer. He may have to change you in order that you can cope with the outcome of your prayers.

'Lord I want to do great things for you.' 'O.K.' God answers, 'but I need to change you first or the pressure will destroy you.'

Or 'God please change my partner.' And God says 'O.K. but I'll have to change you first or else your **changed** partner won't put up with you.'

Have you ever noticed it often gets worse before it gets better!

When we understand this principle it becomes easier to understand the words of

> James. 1:2-4, *"Consider it pure joy my brothers, whenever you face trials of many kinds, because you know that the testing of your faith develops perseverance. Perseverance must finish its work so that you may be mature and complete not lacking anything."*

These words cannot make sense unless you understand that you are securely rooted and established in God's love – he will never let you down.

God wants to bless us but not just to bless us; He has a purpose for us, as children of God, on this earth. He wants us to play our part in His great commission and we do this best as we learn to operate off faith rather than feelings.

This incubation period is where our faith is tested. But we must realise that although everything in our material world may suggest the opposite; we are in fact pregnant with something that is created in another realm, namely - the fourth dimension, the realm of the spirit.

God has never given up creating. In the time of Jesus on earth he was creating new eyes, new limbs, new hearts and new lives. And wherever the gospel is accepted at face value he has been doing the same ever since.

We pray and then God begins to create and form the embryo so that it is ready for the birth. Real faith is not wavering when God **appears** to be late with the answer. The practical outworking of faith is therefore, trusting God implicitly with the timing of the answer. So God says, "pray" to His church; gives us hundreds of promises if we will pray but by and large we still do not pray. Real faith is **doing** because we have believed. Maturity is doing what you know to be right even when you don't feel like doing what you know to be right.

> *"Do not become weary in doing good for at the proper time you will reap a harvest if you do not give up."* Galatians 6:19

The Ark was created long before Noah built it!

David was king long before he became king!

The Son of God was on our earth long before He came to our earth!

Abraham was **"The father of many"** long before Sarah gave birth to his **firstborn** Isaac!

The answer to your prayer is often created and waiting in heaven long before you see it on earth.

This is why the prophetic word of God is creative. When God speaks through His word it comes to pass and when God truly speaks through a person it also comes to pass. For God, *"Calls things that are not as if they were."* And He does this because where He is, they already are. Listen: *"Nothing is impossible for God."*

> The Bible says of Abraham *Rom.4:20-21, "Yet he did not waver through unbelief regarding the promise of God, but was strengthened in his faith and gave glory to God, being fully persuaded that God had power to do what he has promised."*

We do not waver because of what we do not see; rather we build in the realm of the spirit knowing that which is spirit will take on matter and materialise in our natural realm.

God has given his church access to the fourth dimension so that we can subdue again, the things that are in a lesser dimension. Out of all that God created in the spirit realm or the natural realm; man was His crowning glory because only man was made in the image of God.

After God had created man He said these words to him, in

> Gen.1:28, *"God blessed them and said to them, 'Be fruitful and increase in number; fill the earth and subdue it. Rule over the fish of the sea and the birds of the air and over every living creature that moves on the ground."*

Man was given dominion over the things of the third dimension; in Christ we can assert that dominion once again, in order that we can advance the "Kingdom of God".
This is God's intention for His church. We must rise up again in the authority that He has invested in us and take dominion over this fallen third dimension. But we will only

do it to the degree that we make contact with heaven and draw from the fourth dimension. Above all we must above all be a people who keep the commands to love, who pray and who listen to God's voice.

Chapter 20

NOW WOULD BE
A GOOD TIME TO DIE

So, here we are at the end of the book. Once the Royal law is in place we can then interpret scripture from the foundation of 'loving at God's intended level. To reach our full potential in Christ we simply must realise that we are commanded to love at God's intended level.

Teacher and Author Myles Munroe said, 'The potential of everything is related to its purpose for being!'

Be determined to ask yourself, 'what is your purpose for being?' Resolve that the answer will be, to love God and enjoy him forever!

We must be careful not to pass Holy Ghost revelation through the sieve of our minds to the degree that we undermine everything that God wants to do in and through us. Death is followed by resurrection and the resurrected life is energised and inspired by the Holy Spirit rather than the soul.

"The work of God is this: to believe in the one he has sent." John 6:29

If Christ lives in you then the fact is you may still think you are a nobody but it is undeniable that you have a somebody living in you.

Nobody can make you feel inferior without your consent! *(Eleanor Roosevelt)*

If you can truly see yourself as God sees you and love yourself accordingly you will learn to see others as God sees them and love them accordingly. Everything is based on the condition of the human heart and the human heart in terms of its relation to God.

Once you believe in God and have been crucified with Christ you cannot continue to sin. This does not mean that you can't or won't sin. What it does mean is that you can find no peace and no comfort until you discontinue in your sin. There is no happiness in sin; therefore, the child of God will desperately want to be rid of sin!

In order for the dream and vision to come to pass you must die to the dream and vision. While ever it remains the driving force in your life you are susceptible to sin. You can't defend your vision in your own strength. You must die then the subsequent resurrection will give you the wherewithal to see the dream and vision comes to pass. A dream may well be vague to detail whereas a vision is clear on detail! A death allows you to see the detail and plan to see it fulfilled.

The greatest truth in the universe is the truth that God loves you. Wow! To truly know this is the liberty that all mankind is seeking. We should understand that feeling forsaken is a prerequisite to truly being used by God. Jesus himself felt as though he had been forsaken!

God can only bring victory through his resurrection life so it is obvious that we will only know true depth if we have died. Object confusion is a path that you will pass down before your vision will come to pass. Be warned if you want it bad enough you will have to tread the pathway of forsakenness. It is God who achieves through us and the more we have died to self the more he will achieve.

Therefore, it is absolutely necessary that we face death. The great paradox is that death actually allows us to enjoy what God is doing and not the opposite! If you allow God to put you to death you will rise to freedom my friend and begin to feel and taste your purpose for living.

What is God's will? Surrender...

Unconditional grace, mercy, love and forgiveness mean just that they have absolutely no conditions. In order to GET these unconditional benefits we must:
> *"But seek first his kingdom and his righteousness, and all these things will be given to you as well."* Matthew 6:33

The trial that brings death may well be the test - albeit in disguise - that will bring life. Only the Spirit can reveal that life comes to the believer through the death of the believer. Your purpose is centred in dying in order to start living. God knows that in order to experience the resurrected life you must be convinced of the necessity of the death. Oh the profound - wisdom of God!

True life can only be perceived the other side of death. Faith is the magnet that draws true life into our experience until we make it our own. Death is experienced by the living in the here and now when they reckon themselves dead.....

Fear is a thing of the past for the person who dies to self. Such a person is a walking definition of freedom. While ever you hold off death you will have to face it. But having faced it in Christ you will never have to face it again.

Most of our fears are based on a perception of the loss of things that are not essential. Yet, once we have defeated these foes our potential becomes staggering.

We must raise the profile of our potential!

God is your source so the Devil wants to separate you from God - at the same time God wants to separate you from THE WORLD, THE FLESH and THE DEVIL in order that he can heal your memories and free you from bondage.

Our vision must begin with the end in mind. Potential is linked to its source, so if our potential is linked to the source of our life, namely, God, then we can raise the profile of our potential to link into what God has told us he will do!

Come to that place of surrender; that place of wild abandonment.

Look again at Jesus commands to love –then, look again and again and again until the realisation dawns. In so doing you will cultivate God's greatest requirement for your life and learn the art of navigation before you get into the storm.

Your dreams are about to come true if only you can realise that if you want to do that, *walk in all the promises of God* you will have to do this - *keep God's commands to love at his required level.*

As I layed awake on the operating table having my heart operated on I didn't realise that I was about to die. No, it wasn't a physical death but it was the death of me. However, it was only in dying that I found out what living really was. A part of me died and a part of me began to live – it was an outworking of the divine exchange.